*The Roman Catholic Church
in the United States*

By the same author

WORLD RELIGIONS

The

Roman Catholic Church

in the

United States

A Guide to Recent Developments

by

BENSON Y. LANDIS

E. P. DUTTON & CO., INC.

NEW YORK   1966

111587

Grateful acknowledgment is made to the following for permission to quote from copyright material:

Daniel Callahan, *The Mind of the Catholic Layman*. Copyright © 1963 Daniel Callahan. Reprinted by permission of the publisher, Charles Scribner's Sons.

The Christian Century Foundation for an editorial: "Browbeating the Protestants," from the October 11, 1928, issue of *The Christian Century*. Copyright 1928 Christian Century Foundation. Reprinted by permission.

Commonweal: "The Status of Women" by Rosemary Lauer, December 20, 1963; article by John Cogley, January 10, 1964; "Academic Freedom" by Leslie Dewart, April 3, 1964; editorial "Responsible Parenthood," June 5, 1964.

Raymond J. Gallagher, in "Catholic Social Services." *Social Work Year Book 1960* (New York: National Association of Social Workers, 1960), p. 136.

Look: "Democratic Forecast: A Catholic in 1960," March 3, 1959. Reprinted by permission of *Look*.

Statistics from *The Official Catholic Directory*, 1965. Reprinted by permission of the publisher, P. J. Kenedy & Sons.

The Pilot: Article by Monsignor Lally from the August 1, 1964, issue of *The Pilot*. Reprinted by permission.

Your Sunday Missal. Reprinted by permission of the Catholic Book Publishing Co.

To the Memory of Good Pope John (John XXIII, 1881–1963),
  who
In the spirit of a rural pastor became the servant of the serv-
  ants of God;
Opened windows, built bridges, removed walls, thus encour-
  aging searches for renewal and unity;
Spoke to and was heard by many people of many faiths
  throughout the world;
Became one of the most influential men of his time,
This book is dedicated.

My vocation is to build bridges.—Attributed to John XXIII.

We intend to continue the ongoing dialogue.—Paul VI, in coronation address, 1963.

Dialogue has replaced diatribe.—John C. Heenan, Archbishop of Westminster, 1962.

The Roman Catholic Church has moved further in the past three years than Protestantism has moved in 50 years.—Samuel Miller, dean of the Harvard Divinity School, 1963.

Foreword

Prior to the election of Angelo Roncalli as Pope John XXIII in the fall of 1958, there was relatively little interest in things Catholic, much less in a "Catholic viewpoint." Within the four and one-half years of his reign as Pontiff of the Roman Catholic Church, new words became prominent in daily conversations among clergy and laymen of all faiths, words such as ecumenical, dialogue, *aggiornamento* (updating) and liturgy.

The author of this book, a Protestant layman, was committed to "dialogue with mutual respect" long before the words attained present vogue. His personal interest and his involvement in the *Yearbook of American Churches* have brought him in contact with all the major religious bodies. These have prepared and enabled him to study objectively and evaluate with respect what has taken place in the Christian milieu, historically, currently, and especially in the light of the Second Vatican Council. Hence his appraisals should contribute in a practical way to dialogue.

In this short book a considerable number of the more important issues and developments are presented with concise clarity and perspective. He recognizes the Church as an organizational structure as well as a "community of the faithful"; he portrays lay initiative, various movements within the Church, and focus of Christian life around the liturgy (the form Christian worship of God takes) in the same straightforward manner as he presents the Second Vatican Council and its ramifications on various polemics and matters that have strained Christian relations. There is careful distinction between Church and the people who compose the Church, between the teachings of the Church and those who may or may not be implementing those teachings. Thus the human element within the Church structure is clearly and fairly presented.

Dr. Landis, who has at times been called one of the most "catholic" of Protestant laymen, here demonstrates both his knowledge and his workmanship. One who has such interests and perspectives provides a good introduction and orientation for persons of all faiths.

Thomas B. Kenedy, Editor
THE OFFICIAL CATHOLIC DIRECTORY

Contents

This book presents a description of general characteristics of the Roman Catholic Church, followed by appraisals of important recent changes and developments. It is prepared for persons of all faiths and of none. The work is written by a layman with a long and keen interest in religious bodies. It is also by a Protestant who has endeavored systematically to study the Roman Catholic Church for many years.

The emphasis is on recent developments with no special effort to show differences between the Roman Catholic Church and other religious bodies. However, the differences will in many instances be evident to those familiar with other faiths. There are accents on events in the United States, along with due regard for those of the Church at large.

The Roman Catholic Church is an international institution. It is not only the largest Church in Christendom, but also the one with more adherents than any non-Christian religion. Its official language is Latin. It uses a comprehensive liturgical form of worship, with all words under the control of the Pope, who is the Supreme Head of an organization hierarchical in nature. Its central administration is called the Curia, which is often called the largest religious bureaucracy in the world. The Church has a priesthood which has received a relatively uniform education. It functions in well-organized parishes. Church attendance is a well-established practice among the members. The Church has broad responsibility for education, family life, and social life. Much of the Church's work is done by well-disciplined organizations known as "Orders." For example, all but a small proportion of the Catholic colleges and universities in this nation have been established and are now maintained by Orders, whose nature and activities are described in Chapter 1.

The various discussions, events, movements here presented have been chosen by the author. The interpretations of the meanings of the broad information assembled are also his. Among his personal conclusions, which are given without any intent of finality of judgment, are these:

Many things are in flux. There has been a succession of recent changes, related to one another. These have significance at variance with many popular impressions of the Roman Catholic Church in the United States. In some circles it has been customary to say that the Roman Catholic Church is highly or unduly authoritarian, rigid, exclusive, monolithic, or even monarchic. However, recent months and years have resulted in quite different informed opinions, without as well as within, the Roman Catholic Church.

Certain of the personal observations and appraisals made in this work may be briefly stated here. There is good evidence of:

Wide commitment to reading of the Bible by the laity; a continuing process of new translation of the Scriptures; acceptance by a bishop in Scotland, with Papal approval, of a well-known version of Scripture made by American Protestant scholars—the Revised Standard Version—with only a few changes to which the Protestants readily agreed. (This version is accepted in Scotland for reading, not for use in the Mass.)

Broad liturgical movements encouraging understanding and participation of the laity, culminating in use of the vernacular instead of the traditional Latin in many parts of the Mass.

Numerous declarations by officials of the Church on public and social policies, probably more specific than those of any other large religious body in the United States.

Well-established systems of education under Church auspices, from elementary to graduate levels.

New experiments in many communities of "dual enrollment" of parish school pupils in public schools, for instruction in some subjects.

Strong institutions of social welfare (often called "charities" by Catholics) under Church administration, with complete social service for handicapped and dependent children.

Much use of mass communication, with the use of modern techniques, and of language departing from that of the traditional Thomism.

A most remarkable contribution to his Church by the public life and work of John F. Kennedy.

Increasing recognition of population problems and family responsibility, with churchmen of high rank calling for review of the Church's opposition to the use of contraceptives for purposes of birth control.

Approval by bishops of the United States of a policy of religious liberty for all; a ferment of discussion of the issue in the rest of the world.

The unusual influence in the United States, as well as throughout the world, of "Good Pope John," who convened the Second Vatican Council, 1963–1965.

The results of the Second Vatican Council in "updating" the Church, in encouraging critical self-examination, and in bettering relationships with other religious bodies.

Sanction by Popes John XXIII and Paul VI of "dialogue" with mutual respect between Roman Catholics and leaders of other faiths, thus relaxing interreligious tensions of long standing.

Establishment of "ecumenism" as worldwide official policy, thus encouraging systematic search for new understanding and cooperation.

Decentralizing forces in a previously highly centralized body, including a higher degree of freedom for the laity.

Marked movement toward making the Church more than ever an "open" organization—with debate of dilemmas and contradictions for all interested to notice—and with divisions on many current issues into "progressive" and "conservative" groups.

In other nations, the same essential problems and issues are present as are here dealt with, but with different settings and situations. The Church in the United States, for example, is in many ways far different from the ultraconservative one of Spain. And the Church of the United States is also much unlike that in the nations in Latin America that were evangelized by the Spanish. In Latin America, there is a poorly educated clergy, and the Church of the United States is giving much assistance to the churches in the nations to the south. In Latin America, too, the rate of population growth is reported to be the highest in the world, and there is pressure of people upon resources in a way unknown in the United States. Social welfare services in the Latin-American churches are not as well developed as those of the United States. The situation in Canada, too, is far different from that of the United States, because there the Roman Catholics are mainly in one section.

Official statistics of the Roman Catholic Church are summarized, and a few comparisons with other bodies in the United States are made. A glossary of terms frequently used in the Catholic Church is included because it has a distinct vocabulary not always familiar to others. A Note on Sources lists titles selected from numerous references. Specific quotations from sources are credited in the Notes at the end of the text.

1

General Characteristics
of the Roman Catholic Church

Important aspects of the beliefs and teachings, form of worship, and kind of organization of the Roman Catholic Church are here given briefly as background for consideration in more detail later of recent discussions and developments.

The Holy Roman Catholic and Apostolic Church is frequently called the Roman Catholic Church or the Catholic Church. This Church recognizes the Bishop of Rome as Pope, as Vicar of Christ on earth, and as visible head and supreme ruler. It traces its origin to Christ's selection of Peter as chief of the Apostles, and regards the Bishop of Rome as Peter's successor. Like many other religious bodies, the Roman Catholic Church was brought to the United States by immigrants from Europe.

Beliefs and Teachings

The beliefs and teachings of the Roman Catholic Church are found in the sources given by Christ himself and through His Apostles. This deposit of faith is sustained by the Holy Scriptures and by tradition. The beliefs are defined and safeguarded by the Pope when he chooses to speak as Head of the Church and says specifically that he speaks on a matter of faith and morals. When such a declaration is made by the Pope, it is regarded as doctrine revealed by God and is contained in the Sacred Depository of Faith. This is spoken of as "Papal infallibility." It does not mean, and the Pope does not claim, that a Pope cannot do wrong in his ordinary duties.

The essential truths accepted by the Roman Catholic Church are contained in the Apostles' Creed, the Nicene Creed, and the Athanasian Creed. The texts of the two best known of the creeds, the Apostles' and the Nicene, are relatively brief, and read as follows:

THE APOSTLES' CREED

"I believe in God, the Father almighty, creator of heaven and earth; and in Jesus Christ, His only Son, our Lord; who was conceived by the Holy Spirit, born of the Virgin Mary, suffered under Pontius Pilate, was crucified, died, and was buried. He descended into hell: the third day he arose again from the dead; he ascended into heaven, sits at the right hand of God, the Father almighty; whence he shall come to judge the living and the dead.

"I believe in the Holy Spirit, the holy Catholic Church, the communion of saints, the forgiveness of sins, the resurrection of the body, and life everlasting. Amen."

THE NICENE CREED

"I believe in one God, the Father almighty, maker of heaven and earth, and of all things visible and invisible. And I believe in one Lord, Jesus Christ, the only-begotten Son of God. Born of the Father before all ages. God of God, light of light, true God of true God. Begotten, not made, of one substance with the Father. By whom all things were made. Who for us men and for our salvation came down from heaven. And he became flesh by the Holy Spirit of the Virgin Mary: and was made man. He was also crucified for us, suffered under Pontius Pilate, and was buried. And on the third day he rose again according to the Scriptures. He ascended into heaven and sits at the right hand of the Father. He will come again in glory to judge the living and the dead. And of his kingdom there will be no end. And I believe in the Holy Spirit, the Lord and Giver of life, who proceeds from the Father and the Son. Who together with the Father and the Son is adored and glorified, and who spoke through the prophets. And one holy, Catholic and Apostolic Church. I confess one baptism for the forgiveness of sins. And I await the resurrection of the dead. And the life of the world to come. Amen."

There is, also, a general formula of doctrine, arranged in the profession of faith, that must receive the assent of all those who become members of the Church. This profession includes rejection of doctrines that have been declared to be wrong by the Church, a promise of obedience to the authority of the Church in matters of faith, and acceptance of a statement of belief that reads:

"One only God, in three divine persons, distinct from, and equal to, each other—that is to say, the Father, the Son, and the Holy Spirit.

"The Catholic doctrine of the Incarnation, Passion, Death, and Resurrection of our Lord Jesus Christ; and the personal union of the two Natures, the divine and the human; the divine maternity of the Most Holy Mary, together with her spotless virginity.

"The true, real, and substantial presence of the Body and Blood, together with the Soul and Divinity of our Lord Jesus Christ, in the most holy Sacrament of the Eucharist.

"The seven sacraments instituted by Jesus Christ for the salvation of mankind; that is to say, Baptism, Confirmation, Eucharist, Penance, Extreme Unction, Orders, Matrimony.

"Purgatory, the resurrection of the dead, everlasting life.

"The primacy, not only of honor, but also of jurisdiction, of the Roman Pontiff, successor of St. Peter, Prince of the Apostles, Vicar of Jesus Christ; the veneration of the saints and of their images; the authority of the apostolic and ecclesiastical traditions, and of the Holy Scriptures, which we must interpret, and understand, only in the sense which our holy mother the Catholic Church has held and does hold; and everything else that has been defined and declared by the sacred canons, and by the General Councils, and particularly by the Holy Council of Trent, and delivered, defined, and declared by the General Council of the Vatican, especially concerning the primacy of the Roman Pontiff, and his infallible teaching authority."

SACRAMENTS

The seven sacraments recognized by the Roman Catholic Church, listed above, are now described as follows:

Baptism, which "cleanses from original sin," is administered to both infants and adults by pouring of water and pronouncement of the prescribed ritual. Baptism is a condition of membership, whether it is received in infancy or in later years. When a person is baptized, his name is officially registered as a Roman Catholic, and it is generally so retained unless there is a formal act of renunciation of such membership by the person.

Confirmation, through which the "Holy Spirit is received," is by the laying on of hands by the bishop and by anointing of the holy chrism (oil) in the form of a cross.

The Eucharist is that which "contains the body and blood, soul and divinity, of the Lord Jesus Christ, under the appearance of bread and wine," and is received fasting for one hour. It is given to the laity in the form of a wafer.

Penance is the sacrament through which sins committed after baptism are forgiven.

Orders is that by which priests and bishops are ordained.

Extreme Unction (recently renamed the Anointing of the Sick) is the sacrament by which the seriously ill receive succor by anointing with holy oil and prayers offered by a priest.

Matrimony unites a man and woman in lawful marriage, which is not to be "dissolved by any human power."

The moral obligations of Roman Catholics are found in the Ten Commandments of God (Exodus 20:1–17), and in the precepts of the Church, summarized as follows: The Church commands its members to attend Mass on Sundays and on Holy Days of Obligation; to fast and to abstain on the days appointed; to confess to a priest at least once a year; to receive the Holy Eucharist at Easter time; to contribute toward the support of pastors; and to observe the regulations of the Church with respect to marriage.

THE MYSTICAL BODY OF CHRIST

The Roman Catholic concept of the Church is thoroughly stated in its teaching of "the Mystical Body." The Church is the Mystical Body of Christ. The members are those baptized, with the exception of those who have separated themselves by apostasy, heresy, or schism. The term "Mystical" is used to distinguish it from the body of Christ that ascended into heaven, and from the "Eucharistic Body" of Christ which is received in the Sacrament of the Mass.

Scriptural bases of the doctrine are found in 1 Corinthians 12:12–31, of which a few lines are quoted here: "For as the body is one and has many members; and all the members of the body, whereas there are many, yet one body: so also is Christ. For in one Spirit were we all baptized into one body. . . . Now God hath set the members, every one of them, in the body as it hath pleased him. . . ."

The living Church thus has a dual aspect, both a spiritual and a physical nature. It is both an institution on earth and an invisible union with Christ.

Pius XII, writing the encyclical *Mystici Corporis Christi* (*Mystical Body of Christ*, 1943), generalized: "If we would define and describe the true Church of Jesus Christ —which is the One Holy, Catholic, Apostolic Roman Church—we shall find nothing more noble, more sublime, or more divine than the expression 'the Mystical Body of Christ'—an expression which springs from and is, as it were, the fair flowering of the repeated teaching of the Sacred Scriptures and the Holy Fathers. . . . It is the will of Jesus Christ that the whole body of the Church, no less than the individual members, should resemble Him . . . The Spirit of Christ is the channel through which all the gifts, powers, and extraordinary graces found superabundantly in the Head as in their service flow into all the members of the Church, and are perfected daily in them according to the place they hold in the Mystical Body of Jesus Christ."

"OUTSIDE THE CHURCH, NO SALVATION"

The Roman Catholic Church also teaches: "Ex Ecclesia, nulla sallus" (Outside the Church there is no salvation). Does this mean that the salvation of a soul is possible only for those who are formally members of the Roman Catholic Church? The Catholic Church teaches that the ordinary means of salvation are membership in that Church and serious performance of the requirements of membership. However, a decree of the Sacred Congregation of the Holy Office, 1949, reads in part as follows: "We are taught that there is no salvation outside the Church. However, this dogma must be understood in the sense in which the Church herself understands it. . . . That one may obtain eternal salvation, it is not always required that he be incorporated into the Church actually as a member, but it is necessary that at least he be united to her by desire and longing. . . . This desire need not always be explicit, as it is with catechumens [persons receiving instruction prior to membership]; but when a person is involved in invincible ignorance God accepts also an implicit desire, so called because it is included in that good disposition of soul whereby a person wishes his soul to conform to the will of God." In less formal language, the glossary in the National Catholic Almanac, 1964, states: "Those, however, who remain outside the visible unity of the Catholic Church through no grave fault of their own, and do not know it is the true Church, can be saved by making use of the graces which God gives them." A Catholic layman once said to the writer of this book that he understood his Church to teach that those who love God and sincerely seek to do His will are in some way related to the Church that Jesus Christ founded and thus can be saved.

Worship

The main public form of worship in the Roman Catholic Church is by liturgy officially approved by the Pope. Worship is expressed not only in the Mass, but in the administration of sacraments (already described above under "Beliefs and Teachings"), the Divine Office, and the sacramentals.

The Mass, or the formal worship service in the parish,

is customarily arranged at hours convenient for members of the parish. The more important Sunday service, the sung Mass, is celebrated between 10:00 A.M. and noon. At this, some parts of the liturgy are sung by the officiating clergyman and other portions by the choir. The other such services without music are called recited Masses. The number of Sunday services may vary up to seven or more in a parish, depending upon the location, size, and conditions. Vespers are also sung on Sunday afternoons and evenings. Mass is said daily, and special services are held on holydays.

The liturgy is uniform for all churches and has been said mainly in Latin, except in the churches in the United States named "Eastern Rite," which have the right to use their own liturgies. However, even when the Mass was said mainly in Latin, the sermons, instructions, and Scripture have always been in the language spoken by members of the parish. The Second Vatican Council authorized, with approval of the Pope, broad use of the vernacular in most parts of the Mass and administration of the sacraments, a process begun in the United States in 1964, and being promptly implemented. (This is more fully documented in Chapter 3, "Liturgical Movements," and Chapter 14, "Second Vatican Council.")

The Divine Office is that approved daily service of prayer and praise offered for Catholics and the Church by priests and by the members of the religious orders who have taken solemn vows. The Office consists of prayers, Scripture, readings from the lives of the saints, and writings of theologians. The Breviary is the name of the book used for the Office. Whoever uses the Breviary prays in the name of the Church.

The Sacramentals are the rites, acts, prayers, and objects used in order to obtain temporal and especially spiritual benefits. The people obtain these benefits through the faith brought to their use, and through the prayers which the Church offers for those who use them. Some common Sacramentals are the crucifix, blessed palms, candles, medals, scapulars, holy water; and certain special forms of prayer and ceremonial, including the sign of the cross.

The Church encourages private devotions of its members that are related to the expression in the liturgy. Among the types of private devotions that have the Church's approval are meditation, retreats, visits to the Blessed Sacrament in the church, examination of conscience, prayer for aid to the Virgin Mary (especially by means of a rosary), Stations of the Cross, devotions to the Blessed Mother of God in the month of May, and in honor of the Sacred Heart in June. Churches are open daily for personal devotions and for confessions.

The liturgy is arranged in a systematic "Liturgical Year." It is composed of two cycles which run concurrently. One focuses on the principal events in the life of Christ and the mysteries of man's redemption (the temporal cycle); the other celebrates the feasts of the saints, and is called the sanctoral cycle.

The first one emphasizes aspects of the life of the Christian in a series of the seasons:

Advent accents penance, in preparation for the coming of Christ's birth.

Christmas, when union with Christ is sought through reform of one's own life.

Epiphany, the duty of all men to seek salvation through Christ.

Septuagesima and Lent, the need for prayer and penance, to make reparation to God for one's sins and to obtain the help of God.

Holy Week, the mystery of redemption, suffering, and death to sin.

Easter, resurrection from a state of sin to one of grace. Pentecost, cooperation with the Holy Spirit.

Holy days of obligation in the United States are those when Catholics are bound to attend Mass and to refrain from servile work, as follows:

All Sundays of the year.
Jan. 1. Octave of the Birth of Jesus.
Ascension Day, the 40th day after Easter.
Aug. 15. The Assumption.
Nov. 1. All Saints' Day.
Dec. 8. The Immaculate Conception.
Dec. 25. Christmas.

The rules with respect to abstinence and fast are summed up as follows:

Abstinence means refraining from use of flesh meat and of juice or soup therefrom. Butter, cheese, eggs, and seasoning of foods are permitted. Abstinence is obligatory for all Catholics age seven and over. Abstinence is prescribed every Friday unless it is also a holyday. Days of abstinence, complete, are: Fridays; Ash Wednesday; Holy Saturday, all day, but the bishop may dispense; Vigils of Immaculate Conception, and Christmas, with December 23 or 24, optionally. Days of partial abstinence are: Ember Wednesdays and Saturdays; Vigils of Pentecost.

The rules on fasting require the taking of no more than one full meal a day, but one may take a small amount of nourishment two other times a day. Days of fast are: All weekdays of Lent; Ember Days; Vigils of Pentecost, Immaculate Conception, December 7; Christmas (or December 23 or 24, optionally).

Organization

The organization of the Church is headed by the Bishop of Rome, as Pope. His authority is supreme in matters of faith and morals and in administration of the affairs of the Church. Next to the Pope is the College of Cardinals, who now number 102. These are advisers of the Pope, who administer archdioceses or serve him in the administrative and other agencies of the Church in Rome. On the death of a Pope, the cardinals elect a successor by secret ballot by a two-thirds vote. Until a successor is named, authority is vested in the body of cardinals.

The administration of the Church immediately under the Pope is named the Curia. It consists of Congregations, Tribunals, Offices, and still other units. These are numerous, and only a portion are named below:

Congregations include:

The Holy Office, which guards the teaching of faith and morals. It may examine books submitted and may prohibit the reading by members of certain titles by issuing periodically a list of such known as the Index. A member of the Church may, however, request from a diocesan bishop permission to read a book prohibited by Church law by addressing a letter stating the reason for seeking the permission.

The Council, which has general charge of the discipline of the Catholic people and of the diocesan clergy, that is, those not members of orders. The Congregation of the Council is not to be confused with an assembly of all the bishops of the Church which may be called by the Pope, as for example, the Second Vatican Council, 1962–1965.

Affairs of Religious, which decides matters related to the numerous religious orders.

Sacred Rites, which supervises observance of all rites and ceremonials.

Seminaries and Universities, which regulate all matters pertaining to theological seminaries and colleges and universities.

Propagation of the Faith, which has full charge of Catholic missions and all affairs related thereto.

The Tribunals include the Sacred Rota, which is a court of appeal. It is especially known for its jurisdiction in cases involving marriage, including requests for decrees of nullity.

The Offices include the Secretariat of State, which handles the relationships between the Holy See and civil powers.

Commissions include those on Biblical Studies, on Liturgy, on Revision of the Code of Canon Law, on Motion Pictures, Radio, and Television.

The organization in the United States is headed by an Apostolic Delegate, archbishops, of whom some are cardinals, bishops, and clergy in parishes and other activities.

Bishops are appointed by the Consistorial Congregation in Rome, with the approval of the Pope. Priests are ordained by bishops (see "Clergy," below).

In the local parish, the priest is in charge, subject to the bishop. Appointment to a parish is solely under the control of the bishop. Only the priest may conduct worship and administer the sacraments offered in the parish. He may in a large parish have numerous assistants. Only the bishop may confirm new members. Lay persons are consulted in the management of the affairs of the parish, and there are often numerous local organizations among men, women, and youth.

Usually all parish income received is handled by the priest. This income is from such as plate collections, offerings for baptisms, marriages, Masses, special drives and events for charities or education. The priest may retain personally only the fixed amount assigned by the diocese for his salary, which is uniform throughout the diocese. The parish also usually provides the priest or priests with a dwelling and at least a portion of ordinary living and professional expenses. This may include utilities, automobile expense, and books or other literature essential for a clergyman's parish duties.

For promotion of unity in Catholic work in the United States, the bishops organized the National Catholic Welfare Conference, first named the National Catholic War Council, in 1917. This agency, with headquarters in Washington, has numerous departments and related organizations emphasizing education, information, social welfare, international cooperation, and legal matters.

The missionary work of the Church in the United States is promoted by various societies, including those with special programs among Negroes and American Indians. For foreign missions, the representative organization in the United States is the Society for Propagation of the Faith, the official organization of the Holy See, with headquarters in Rome and a national office in New York.

Clergy

Young men prepare for the priesthood by studying in divinity schools and theological seminaries maintained by the dioceses and religious orders. Beginning with the first small seminary in Baltimore shortly after American Independence, the Church has developed literally hundreds of institutions for preparing the clergy. (See Chapter 7, "Education.") On taking a vow of chastity a student in a seminary, usually called a seminarian, is ordained a subdeacon by a bishop. After a period he is made a deacon, then a priest. The priest may conduct worship and administer sacraments. The deacon may only by authorization, in exceptional circumstances, preach and administer sacraments. In 1964, bishops were granted discretionary authority to appoint married deacons of mature age (see Chapter 14, "Second Vatican Council").

Priests are divided into two groups, but both go through the same procedure for ordination. Diocesan priests are attached to a diocese and may have private property like other citizens. Regular priests are members of orders, renounce private property, and live under the rule of the order. They are called "regular" because subject to the rule. If a member of an order becomes a parish priest, he must manage parish affairs as the bishop directs. However, the diocesan priests are generally in charge of parishes, and the regular priests are usually in educational, missionary, social service, or other special work. In the United States in 1965, there were 58,632 priests, of whom 35,925, or about 60 percent, were diocesan.

There are common obligations for all priests. They must recite the Divine Office daily; show respect to superiors, continue to study, and wear a distinct garb. They may not marry. They are forbidden to engage in certain public amusements. They may not hold public office for pay. They may not speculate in securities. The requirements of the priesthood are thus rather formal and rigid. However, the obligations have been freely undertaken.

Among the many local duties of the parish priest, in addition to conducting public worship, are to visit the sick; prepare children and others for their first Confession, Holy Communion, and Confirmation; protect church property from unbecoming activities. He must announce banns of marriage, perform marriage ceremonies, hold funeral services, lead any public procession outdoors. He is entitled only to regulated and customary fees for voluntary services and for administration of sacraments. He must ordinarily reside near his church. He is usually in charge of only one parish.

Religious Orders

An important characteristic of the Church is its reliance on the devotion and labor of the members of religious orders. These are of two types: First, there are the orders in which the members take solemn vows of obedience, poverty, and chastity. Second, there are the religious congregations in which the members take simple vows, and may hold private property.

An order is governed by a superior, who is represented by subordinates or councils of communities, if the order is formed in more than one nation. The clerical members of orders are ordained, and their ordination is altogether under the control of a bishop. The order may also have lay members who take the vows but are not conducted into the priesthood. They assist in caring for the ordinary affairs of the orders.

Members of brotherhoods and sisterhoods take vows but are not ordained. Many of these persons are engaged in educational, health, social service, and related work.

The constitution and rule of every order must have the approval of the Sacred Congregation of Religious of the Holy See.

Among the well-known and large orders for men, with membership reported in the United States are:

Society of Jesus, members called Jesuits, with 8,105 clergy, and 680 brothers.

Friars Preachers, members called Dominicans, with 1,379 clergy, and 158 brothers.

Friars Minor, members called Franciscans, with 3,078 clergy, and 669 brothers. Two separate divisions of Friars Minor also have smaller numbers of members in the United States.

Order of St. Benedict, members called Benedictines, with 2,833 clergy, and 552 brothers.

Among the many of those for women are Sisters of St. Francis (of Assisi) with 77 congregations in the United States, and the Sisters of the Third Order of St. Dominic with 32 congregations in the United States. Both of these do extensive educational and hospital work.

There were 192,325 unordained members of religious orders in the United States in 1965, of whom 12,271 were brothers and 179,554 sisters.

There are "Third Orders Secular" whose members are lay persons. They are so named because of their origin. St. Francis of Assisi founded the friars (first order); St. Clare organized the Poor Clares (second order); then St. Francis formed an order of laymen (third order). These lay people live by the usual occupations of the community at large. Their general duties are to transmit to the world something of the religious spirit of the cloisters. Among the best known of the third orders today are those of the Franciscans, Carmelites, Dominicans, Benedictines, and Augustinians.

The Encyclicals

The encyclical is one form of communication used by the Popes. Some encyclicals receive considerable public attention. They are described here only in general, and many of them are summarized in the chapters that follow in connection with the appropriate subject matter.

The encyclicals may be called letters. They are usually addressed to the bishops of the Church throughout the world, or to the bishops of one nation. Certain of them, for example, have been addressed to the bishops of the United States. Pope John XXIII addressed his letter, *Pacem in Terris* (*Peace on Earth*), 1963, to the bishops and faithful of the world, and also to men of goodwill everywhere, which was without precedent.

Encyclicals have also been defined as essays of advice,

or declarations of guidelines, or statements of major policies. They are expressions of the Church's teaching authority. They are always deserving of the careful attention
of the Church, but, in recent centuries at least, they are
not vehicles declaring dogma on faith and morals having
infallible authority.

Some Popes wrote many encyclicals, others few. Leo
XIII wrote 50; Pius XII, 30; Pius IX, 16; John XXIII, 8.
The Popes decide the subjects and the frequency. They
are probably always written after considerable collaboration or consultation, but the personalities and accents and
ideas of the Popes signing them are revealed by their
styles of expression.

Vatican City

The Pope is the ruler of Vatican City, a territory of
some 108 acres with a population of about 1,000 persons.
It became an independent and sovereign state (or a spe-
cial kind of a state) in 1929, by the terms of the Lateran
Treaty negotiated by the government of Italy and the
Holy See. The area is an almost triangular section of the
City of Rome, on the west bank of the Tiber River. In
Rome there are also important churches that are part of
Vatican City but not in the same territory. The political
freedom of Vatican City, under the Lateran Treaty, is
guaranteed by Italy. Vatican City has its own coins, post-
age, flag, and diplomatic corps (see below). The City has
a citizenship of its own. There are a governor and a lay
council appointed by the Pope. The law is the Canon Law
of the Catholic Church. The Vatican Museum and the
Library are among the most important institutions of their
kind in the world. The large Basilica of St. Peter in Vatican
City is undoubtedly one of the world's most famous
churches.

Politically, Vatican City may be said generally to resemble the earlier and larger Papal States, a large section of central Italy, which the Pope ruled from about 750 to 1870, when Italian nationalism called for a united Italy, and the States came under Italian rule (see Chapter 12, "The Papacy in Modern Perspective"). However, there is no direct connection between Vatican City and the Papal States. By the Treaty of 1929, Italy provided a financial indemnity for its seizure of the former Papal States.

Vatican Diplomacy

Papal diplomacy has been defined as a system "of reciprocal permanent representation which the Papacy has developed over the centuries to expedite through official channels any issue requiring negotiation or consultation with the several states," [1] Father Robert Graham generalizes.

The present Pope, when he was Monsignor Montini in the service of the Holy See, once defined diplomacy in general as the "art of creating and maintaining international order, that is to say, peace." He also defended the Vatican system of diplomacy, because in his opinion it furthers one of the aims of the Church, namely "the universal brotherhood of men."

Roman Catholics are not all in favor of the Vatican diplomatic system. Father Graham reports that strong points are sometimes made against it in Church circles. And after his book was published, at least one prelate called for abolition of the system in a speech at the Second Vatican Council.

Recently there have been at the Holy See twenty-four ambassadors, ten ministers plenipotentiary, and two chargés d'affaires. The Holy See sent reciprocal representatives to most of the states having diplomats at the Vatican. The Vatican representatives abroad are today "always ecclesiastics."

Nations with diplomats at the Vatican are by no means all known as "Catholic states." France is a secular state, according to its constitution, and is "fiercely separationist," but sends a diplomatic mission to the Holy See. Among other nations with diplomats at the Vatican are Great Britain (with the Church of England as the "state church"), India, Japan, Lebanon, United Arab Republic, Turkey, Poland, Netherlands, West Germany, Finland. Public opposition to diplomatic relations on the part of the United States, thinks Father Graham, is based mainly on the prevailing opinion on the separation of church and state.

However, the United States appointed consuls to the Papal States as early as 1797. They were regarded in the United States as mainly commercial representatives, but in the Papal States they were received in the same manner as the consuls from other nations.

President Polk recommended that full diplomatic relations be established with the Papal States in a message to Congress, but the step was not implemented until the Administration of President Buchanan. Jacob L. Martin, the first chargé d'affaires, was instructed by President Buchanan in 1848 to confine his attention to "civil relations with the Papal government, and to extension of commerce." The whole procedure was regarded as highly controversial by the American people. The "nativistic movements" of the time were especially opposed. Finally, Congress in 1867 declined to make an appropriation for the maintenance of the formal relationship, partly because of restrictions on the liberty of Protestant churches in Rome. The absence of an appropriation closed the mission.

No formal letters of notification or recall were ever sent by the United States to the Papal States.

President Roosevelt in 1939 appointed Myron C. Taylor to be his "personal representative to His Holiness the Pope" with the personal rank of ambassador but not with full diplomatic status. Mr. Taylor was a prominent lawyer who became head of the United States Steel Corporation, and was a member of the Protestant Episcopal Church. He served until January, 1950, thus spending about five years under President Roosevelt and five under President Truman. Mr. Taylor's activities had to do mainly with World War II and its aftermath. In October, 1951, President Truman recommended to Congress that General Mark W. Clark, a prominent military officer of World War II, be made "Ambassador Extraordinary and Plenipotentiary to Vatican City." Mr. Truman said that both diplomatic and humanitarian interests of the United States would be served by the appointment. The President thought it would aid in resisting the forces making for the spread of Communism in the world. Public outcry in opposition was intense and prolonged, and General Clark requested that his name be withdrawn. No other nomination has since been made. It seems altogether clear that President Truman and not Vatican City initiated the nomination of General Clark.

2

The Bible

To the Roman Catholics, the Bible not only contains the word of God—it is the word of God. The "primary author" is the Holy Spirit, meaning that human authors composed their works under Divine inspiration.

In terms of literature, the Bible is a collection of varied writings that the Church has recognized as inspired. The term Bible is of both Greek and Latin origin. The writings came early to be called "The Book" because it was regarded as divinely inspired. St. Jerome called the collection "The Divine Library" in the fourth century. The words Scripture, Scriptures, Holy Scripture, Holy Scriptures, are also sometimes used.

Nature of the Literature

The literature is in two parts. The older of the writings, written by Jews, mostly in Hebrew, is named the Old Testament, designating what was written before the coming of Christ. The later writings, probably begun soon after Christ's crucifixion and resurrection, are Greek writings called the New Testament. Both collections are regarded as having the same purpose and character. However, not all truth is revealed by the Bible—tradition is also a method of transmitting God's revelation. This consists of truth handed down verbally by Christ and His Apostles, and communicated through all generations since by the Church in her teaching authority.

The "canon" of the Bible (i.e., the books regarded as most authentic) was determined at about the end of the fourth century. The Council of Trent again specifically named the books regarded as "sacred and canonical" in 1563. These are now 72 books in Roman Catholic editions, 45 in the Old Testament and 27 in the New Testament. The Catholic edition contains books not included by Jews in their Scriptures, and seven books in the Old Testament that Protestants generally list in the Apocrypha. Among the independent Greek and Russian Orthodox churches, the canon is the same as that of the Roman Catholics. Among other Orthodox churches there are variations.

The Old Testament was in the process of writing and compilation during the nine centuries prior to the Christian Era, and the New Testament was probably completed about A.D. 150. Although the Bible is fragmentary, part of a larger body of writing, it is peculiarly of value both for its literary beauty and its power over the lives and works of men.

The Dead Sea Scrolls, manuscripts discovered in 1953 and succeeding years in caves in Palestine, have been of special interest to students of the Bible. Some 1,500 articles and books have already been published concerning them. The scrolls include texts of books of the Old Testament, and portions of these books. They throw light upon a relatively obscure era, the era between the writings of the Old Testament and the New, especially on a religious community, thought by some to be one of the Essenes, mentioned in the New Testament.

Arrangement

The 72 books approved by the Council of Trent are arranged in Roman Catholic Bibles as follows:

Old Testament; Historical Books: The Pentateuch (Genesis, Exodus, Leviticus, Numbers, Deuteronomy), Josue, Judges, Ruth, 1, 2, 3, and 4 Kings, 1 and 2 Chronicles, 1 and 2 Esdras, Tobias, Judith, Esther, and 1 and 2 Machabees.

Didactic Books: Job, Psalms, Proverbs, Ecclesiastes, Canticle of Canticles, Wisdom, Ecclesiasticus.

Prophetical Books: Isaias, Jeremias (including Lamentations), Baruch, Ezechiel, Daniel, Osee, Joel, Amos, Abdias, Jonas, Micheas, Nahum, Habacuc, Sophonias, Aggeus, Zacharias, and Malachias.

New Testament; Historical Books: Gospels According to Matthew, Mark, Luke, and John, and Acts of the Apostles.

Doctrinal Books: The fourteen Epistles of St. Paul (Romans, 1 and 2 Corinthians, Galatians, Ephesians, Philippians, Colossians, 1 and 2 Thessalonians, 1 and 2 Timothy, Titus, Philemon, and Hebrews). The seven Catholic Epistles (James; 1 and 2 Peter; 1, 2, and 3 John; and Jude).

Prophetical Book: The Apocalypse.

Versions

It is well known that the original manuscripts of the authors of the Bible have been lost. The text has come through ancient copies and versions of which a few survive to this day. The Latin Vulgate version was a revision and translation made by St. Jerome about A.D. 383–406, on orders of Pope St. Damascus. The Council of Trent decided that the Vulgate of St. Jerome was the authentic or authoritative text for public readings, disputations, and preachings.

The "basic" English translation is named "The Douay." It was undertaken by English scholars in exile on the Continent of Europe. The New Testament was published at Rheims in 1582 and the Old Testament at Douay in

1609. Bishop Richard Challoner, Vicar Apostolic in London, completed a new English version of the Douay-Rheims Bible in 1750. This became the English Bible most widely used by Catholics in the United States.

The Confraternity of Christian Doctrine, through its Episcopal Committee, published a newly revised New Testament in English in the United States in 1941. It was the result of five years' work by forty-three Catholic scholars. It is popularly called the Confraternity edition or version. The same Committee is proceeding with work on the Old Testament. Portions of the Old Testament (Psalms; Historical Books, Genesis to Ruth; Didactic Books, Job to Ecclesiasticus; Prophetical Books, Isaias to Malachias) have been published between 1948 and 1961. All but a few of the Old Testament books have now been translated, but not all have been published.

Other modern Catholic translations in English include the New Testament by Francis O. Spencer, O.P., 1948; the New Testament by James H. Kleist and Joseph L. Lilly, 1954; The Bible by Ronald Knox, 1955.

Instruction of Members

The Church prohibits its members from use of Bible versions not having approval by its own ecclesiastical authorities. The Church also declares that it alone shall make interpretations of Bible text—and not a priest or a member. The Vatican Council of 1870, reiterating the Council of Trent, said on interpretation of the Bible:

"We, renewing the said decree [of Trent], declare this to be its meaning: that in matters of faith and morals pertaining to the building up of Christian doctrine, that is to be held as the true sense of Sacred Scripture which Holy Mother the Church has held and does hold, to whom it belongs to judge the true sense and interpretation of

Holy Scripture, and therefore it is permitted to no one to interpret the said Scriptures against this sense or, likewise, against the unanimous consent of the Fathers" [the Bishops of the Church].

Encouragement of Bible Reading

The Church does not issue interpretations of each chapter and verse of the Scripture. It does encourage its members to read such portions of the Bible that have not been interpreted, asking that they be read in the light of the total content and purpose of the Bible and the general teachings of the Church. Indeed, indulgences for reading the Bible are granted by the Holy See.

For at least seven decades official encouragement of reading the Bible has been such as to be called the "Biblical movement" or the "Biblical revival." Pope Leo XIII issued an encyclical, *Providentissimus Deus* (*Study of Scripturo*) in 1893. Benedict XV issued one, *Spiritus Paraclitus* (*Holy Scripture*), in 1920. Pius XII wrote *Divino Afflante Spiritu* (*Biblical Studies*) in 1943, exactly fifty years after the one by Leo XIII. Pius XII's letter of 1943 is regarded as of special significance because he specifically authorized Biblical scholars to make use of history, archeology, ethnology, and other sciences in the course of their work. He also bade the scholars in the process of their translations to go not only to Jerome's Latin Vulgate but also to Greek and Hebrew texts. He asked for "close study of the ancient writings of the East."

John XXIII in more recent days called attention to the importance of reading the Scriptures:

"Every day you read papers and books, but do you also take time to read the Holy Scriptures?" (1963, in an address to pilgrims in Rome.)

"If, therefore, we set great store by all the solicitude of

pastoral ministry and if we note its urgency, we feel above all that it is our duty, by continuous action everywhere, to arouse enthusiasm for every revelation of the Holy Book which is given to light the path from childhood to old age." (1958, in a sermon.)

"The widespread growth of Bible study today, especially the circulation of new editions of Holy Scripture, adapted to the needs and degree of learning of the various members of the Church, gives rise to the hope that there will be a renewal of Christian life, nourished at the very fountainhead of Revelation. We therefore cannot but encourage every effort which aims at drawing souls nearer to the Bible, the life-giving source of spiritual doctrine." (In a statement, 1959, on the occasion of the celebration of Bible Week in Rome.)

The Catholic Biblical Association of America, an organization of Biblical scholars and others with related interests, was begun in 1936. Publication of its periodical, *Catholic Biblical Quarterly*, started three years later. In 1962, the Association launched another periodical, *The Bible Today*, for promotion of "popular appreciation of the Word of God." The Association has led in observance of Catholic Bible Sunday, held annually on Septuagesima Sunday (which falls from January 18 to February 22), since 1942. The yearly event was broadened into Catholic Bible Week in 1951.

High interest in the Bible has gone on along with a "liturgical movement" or a "liturgical renewal" (see Chapter 3, "Liturgical Movements"). These are not simply parallel movements—they are interdependent and contribute to each other. "The internal unity of Bible and Liturgy is *the* foundation of today's spiritual life," X. Léon-Dufour, a French theologian declares.[1] The leaders of the liturgical movement strive for a fuller participation of the laity in worship. The liturgy of the Catholic Church, like that of other Christian churches, is based upon the Bible, and includes the public reading of the Bible. This accent has, in turn, given rise to new demands for the wider use of the vernacular in liturgy, and the Vatican Council in 1963 implemented such practice (see Chapter 14, "Second Vatican Council").

The interdependence of Scripture and religious instruction and education is recognized by Roman Catholics striving to improve their methods. "Let us . . . make our pupils hungry for God's holy word," urges J. Hofinger, S.J., in a paper on "How to Use the Bible in Religion Class." [2]

These various events and emphases have revealed schools of thought concerning the Bible in the Church. On the one hand there are the so-called "integrists," those who wish to preserve the integrity of the Roman Catholic faith by means of strict official controls over Biblical scholarship and strong discipline. On the other hand, the "liberals" favor relatively more freedom in Biblical scholarship. It is reported, for example, that among German Catholic leaders there has been a relatively "liberal" view, while Italy is the center of "integrist" positions.

Bible as Bond of Unity

"One solution" to the problems of Catholic missionaries in Africa in developing Bible reading is "the utilization of Protestant translations," wrote Dom Thierry Maertens of the Benedictine Abbey of St. André les Bruges in a report after visiting among Catholic priests in Africa.[3]

Actually, Catholic and Protestant Biblical scholars have been using "common methods and reaching common results" since the publication of the Papal encyclical, *Divino Afflante Spiritu* (*Bible Studies*) in 1943, Luther A. Weigle, chairman of the Committee of Protestant scholars that produced the *Revised Standard Version of the Holy Bible* in 1952, records.[4] Dr. Weigle goes on: "The Bible is coming to be, as it should be, a bond of Christian unity rather than an instrument of division."

For several years Catholic scholars in England and the United States have shown an increasingly appreciative interest in the RSV, which is a revision of the King James Version of 1611 and the American Standard Version of 1901. The editor of *Scripture*, a quarterly periodical of the Catholic Biblical Association, in Great Britain, stated in 1963 that The Revised Standard Version of the Bible, first published in 1952, was then well known and frequently used. He also declared it to be the best translation then available, because it gave him ready access to the original text better than any other translation. He believed that it preserved the great tradition of English Bible language, which had long been established by the Authorized [King James] Version.

For Holy Week in 1963 a book containing meditations was prepared by Vincent A. Yzermans with selected Scripture readings from the Revised Standard Version, by permission of the Division of Christian Education of the National Council of Churches.[5] The volume was published with an introduction by Most Reverend Peter W. Bartholome, Bishop of the Diocese of St. Cloud, Minnesota; also with the bishop's *imprimatur* or permission. The publishers announced that it was the first Catholic book to use lengthy excerpts from text other than that of a "Catholic" Bible.

Perhaps the most significant event in making the Bible a bond of unity instead of a means of division came late in 1963, when a Roman Catholic Archbishop in Scotland, Gordon Gray, requested permission to print, with relatively few changes, a Catholic edition of the Revised Standard Version, for use in private reading by Catholics, but not as part of liturgy. As this is written, Papal approval has been received for the text of the New Testament with alterations satisfactory to the American Protestant translators. It is fully planned that this will result in a Catholic edition of the entire RSV Bible. Protestant scholars in the United States emphasize that the initiative was entirely from the Roman Catholics of Scotland.

The edition of the Revised Standard Version for Roman Catholics was prepared, the Introduction states, by the Catholic Biblical Association of Great Britain. The Association had found that the RSV had been widely acclaimed. For 400 years, the Association reported, Catholics and Protestants had gone their separate ways and had suspected each other's translations. These suspicions, it was stated, were at times well-established. Now, however, both Catholics and Protestants make their translations from "substantially" the same Bible texts.

Catholic scholars of Britain had considered, as early as 1953, the possibility of an edition of the Revised Standard Version acceptable to Catholic readers. Since then, too, there has been a great improvement in relations between the Christian Churches. This change greatly helped to "narrow the margin of differences" between Protestant and Catholic Bible translations.

The English scholars formed a small committee, and established contact with the Standard Bible Committee of the National Council of Churches, which had sponsored the RSV. The idea of the British scholars received a warm welcome in the United States. Further, the British group asked for a minimum number of alterations, only to change that which seemed altogether necessary. A complete list of changes has been listed in the Appendix. The list itself is stated to be evidence of a growth of a mutual understanding among Christians of our time.

The conclusion of the Introduction reads: "May this edition of the New Testament contribute both to the increase of knowledge of God's word and to better understanding between Christians according to the mind of our Savior, who prayed 'that they may be one, even as we are one. John 17:11.'"

This is only one of a number of somewhat similar moves in other parts of the world. There are reports of "experiments" in work on common Catholic and Protestant translations of the Scriptures in France, the Netherlands, Cameroun, and elsewhere. Many Roman Catholic and Protestant clergymen have advocated a unified or common Bible as a means of encouraging cooperation and unity. At least two groups of persons acting unofficially as individuals are working in the United States to produce joint translations of the Scriptures.

3

Liturgical
Movements

Beginning in the late years of the nineteenth century there have been liturgical movements with two specific objectives: to obtain more active participation by lay persons, and to change forms and methods so as to make the liturgy more vital and meaningful. Both these emphases will be interpreted here, with special reference to the Holy Sacrifice, or the Sacrifice of the Mass, generally called simply the Mass. The Mass is the chief act of Roman Catholic worship. "Nothing is so consoling, so piercing, so thrilling, so overcoming, as the Mass," wrote John Cardinal Newman. "It is a great action, the greatest action that can be on earth."

Nature of the Mass

"Christ our High Priest continues to offer Himself daily at the Mass." This is the brief generalization once made by Hugo H. Hoever, a Roman Catholic theologian on the faculty of the University of Notre Dame, in his compilation, *I Pray the Mass*, a brief Sunday Missal.[1] "The sacrifice offered on the altar is essentially the same as that which was offered on Calvary, since it is the same Priest and the same victim." Christ offers Himself "through priests ordained to represent him, i.e., make Him present in our midst. It is important, of course, for us to remember that we should offer ourselves along with Christ at Mass.

The Offertory gifts of bread and wine represent ourselves, our labors and our good resolves."

The Mass is not only the chief act of Catholic worship, "It is also its central function, as the altar is the central object in our churches. The grandest functions of the Liturgy, ordinations, consecrations, benedictions, professions, take place during the celebration of the mystery of the altar. According to St. Thomas, all the sacraments center around the Holy Eucharist. Exposition and Benediction of the Blessed Sacrament are, as it were, a continuance of it. We should, therefore, be quite wrong were we to separate such acts of piety as our communions and our adoration, from the act of the sacrifice; let us accustom ourselves to keep this connection practically in mind by communicating with the priest during holy Mass, and by considering our Lord present in the tabernacle as the saving victim.

"The Liturgy has also for its aim the sanctification of mankind. It is the most fruitful source of those divine graces which, spreading from the Father through Christ, into the members of His Mystical Body, assure to them the divine life of grace."

In order to worship fully, many members use a guide. This is named a "Missal," many editions of which are published for the use of the laity. However, a "People's Mass Book" is meeting the needs of others.

The general reasons for attendance at Mass for Catholics are the same as those of many other religious groups: To unite as a community in giving to God the highest and best form of worship; to express thanks to God; to make reparation for sin; to obtain the blessing of God. Catholics also add, to aid the souls in purgatory and to shorten the time there after their death of those worshiping. Purgatory, in Roman Catholic doctrine, is both a place and a state, sometimes called "for purging." More formally, those who die in a state of grace must suffer for a time in purgatory before they may enter heaven, where they are cleansed of sins for which they have not repented and to make satisfaction for temporal punishment still due them because of their sins.

How the Mass Developed

The Mass of today is the result of centuries of development. Little is known of forms of early Christian worship in the first churches of the Middle East. Many of the first Christians were converts from Judaism, and they undoubtedly to some extent followed the ritual of the Jews. There were readings of psalms, hymns were sung, sermons were preached, prayers were said, and collections were taken for the poor. Collections at church are thus no novelty! Out of these beginnings modern forms developed.

The first prayers said by the priest, at the foot of the altar, are the most recent in origin and came into the Mass only in 1570 by decree of St. Pius V, who then revised the Missal. These prayers were earlier simply the private preparations of the priest for the Mass as he approached the altar.

The Introit, the first portion said by the priest when going up to the altar, was originally a processional psalm chanted by the priest as he entered the sanctuary. The text of the psalm used varies from day to day. The Introits of some of the feasts come from the days of St. Gregory the Great (540–604) one of the "doctors of the Church," and the Pope for whom the Gregorian chant was named.

The offering of incense in sacrifices was practiced in ancient pagan and Jewish worship. St. Ambrose (340–397), also a doctor, records its use in the Mass, and thereafter prayers were formally assigned with the ceremonial. It is usually done only at sung Mass.

The Kyrie Eleison, "Lord Have Mercy," is Greek, and is the only portion of the Western or Latin rite in that language. It originated after the second century.

The Mass is arranged into ordinary or unchangeable prayers and changeable parts that vary from Sunday to Sunday, from season to season, and in accordance with the great feast days of the church year.

The order is as follows:

1. Beginning of the Mass
2. Introit
3. Kyrie
4. Gloria
5. Collects
6. Epistle
7. Gospel
8. Sermon and Creed
9. Offertory Verse
10. Offertory Prayers
11. Secret
12. Preface
13. Canon of the Mass
14. Communion
15. Postcommunion
16. Final Prayers

The Gloria, a canticle of praise, a translation of an ancient hymn in Greek, came into use probably as early as the year 130.

The Collects are prayers expressing man's dependence on God. They are so named because any meeting of clergy and laity was once known as a *collecta* or *collectio*, meaning an assembly.

The Epistle, read before the Gospel, is not always from the Epistles of the Bible. Frequently other parts of the

Bible are read. The reading of epistles at worship surely dates from the early apostolic church.

The Gospel is often designated to be appropriate for a day or season, but many of those that must be read are not so chosen. The arrangement now used is believed to have been originated by St. Jerome (340–420), translator of the Scriptures into the Latin (Vulgate version).

The Sermon and Creed. The sermon, which is now required at all Masses on Sundays and holydays, is often an explanation of the Gospel. It is usually brief and is an element of the Liturgy. The Creed now used is the Nicene, formulated by the Council of Nicaea, 325. A creed is a late addition to the Holy Sacrifice. In ancient years it was a fixed portion of the rite of Baptism only, where the Apostles' Creed is still used. In 1014 Benedict VIII ordered it used after the Gospel. Although its use in the Mass was begun in Spain in the sixth century, the creed is omitted in some Masses.

The Offertory is the approach to the Eucharistic act. In ancient days the people brought the bread and wine for the Sacrifice; later money was collected. There is an Offertory Verse, followed by prayers.

The Secret prayers, said in a low voice, are in nature somewhat similar to the Collects said earlier. They are found in the most ancient liturgies of the Church.

The Preface includes prayers of thanksgiving that prepare for the Consecration. It is followed by the prayer of adoration, the Sanctus.

The Canon of the Mass is that part of the Mass before and after the Consecration. (The word canon means rule or standard, in ecclesiastical usage.) The Church requires that it be said according to a standard to which all must conform. The priest says prayers for the Church, the Pope, the bishop; those for commemoration of the living and for persons whom he wishes especially to commend to God that day; one in which he mentions saints and martyrs, to emphasize communion of the worshipers with them. Words of consecration of bread and wine follow. The priest raises the bread which has become the Sacred Host so that it may be seen by the people; then does the same with the chalice with the consecrated wine. The priest says prayers in commemoration of the dead. The preparation for intimate union with Christ in Holy Communion fittingly includes the Our Father or Lord's Prayer.

The priest in his Communion consumes the consecrated wine, which has become the Precious Blood. This is followed by the Communion of the people who receive only the consecrated bread become the Sacred Host. It is placed into the mouth of the communicants. Up to the twelfth century the people received Communion in two kinds, both bread and wine. With few exceptions Holy Communion is received by persons fasting. (A recent regulation provides that those communing need to fast for only one hour, and water may be taken anytime.) The chalice is purified. The priest then reads the designated Communion Prayer, and the Postcommunion Prayer.

There is a final dismissal and blessing. "Ite, missa est" (Go, the Mass is ended, or Go, it is the dismissal). To this the response is "Deo Gratias" (Thanks be to God). But the people have not gone because in 1570 Pope Pius V added other parts: a short prayer; the blessing; the "Last Gospel," usually the first chapter of the Gospel according to St. John; the Mass then actually ended with a "Deo Gratias."

The Liturgical Commission of the Holy See authorized, effective in 1965, shortening the Mass both at the beginning and at the end. Psalm 42, among the preparatory prayers said by the priest and the server, is dropped. The Last Gospel and the final prayers following it are also eliminated.

Name of the Mass

In early Christian times what is now the Mass was known by other names, including the Lord's Supper, the Breaking of Bread, the Solemnity of the Lord, the Sacrifice, the Holy Liturgy, or the Eucharist.

The English word, the Mass, is derived from the Latin *missa*, coming from the verb *mittere,* to send. It means dismissal, surely a curious designation for a great worldwide liturgy. The word was adopted through ancient experience. In the early liturgy of the church there were two distinct parts. The catechumens, those partly instructed or not yet baptized, were dismissed after the Gospel and sermon. The rest of the faithful stayed through to the end of the liturgy when they were dismissed. There were thus two solemn dismissals. Then somehow the word for dismissal came to mean the service from which the worshipers were dismissed. (The term "sending" is also applicable to the apostolic mission of the Church.)

Kinds of Masses

Among the many kinds of masses are these:

A recited Mass is one celebrated without music; the priest simply reads throughout the service.

A sung Mass is one that is sung by the priest celebrating.

A Solemn sung Mass is one sung by the priest celebrating, assisted by a deacon and a subdeacon.

A Pontifical Mass is one celebrated by a bishop.

A Papal Mass is one in which the Pope is celebrant.

A Requiem Mass is one for the dead.

A Nuptial Mass is one celebrated at or after the wedding ceremony.

There are numerous others celebrated on special occasions or special places. One of these is the Field Mass, celebrated out of doors in time of war or at other times by special permission.

Movements for Renewal

The movements of vitalizing worship and encouraging participation of the laity have several emphases. One centers on study and development of architecture in relation to worship. This has led, in some parishes, to adoption of strikingly new forms of buildings, some being popularly called "modern." The purpose is to erect buildings that help to create the mood of worship. Others stress improved singing by congregations of liturgical music. Others emphasize the development of a deeper appreciation of the total forms of worship throughout the Church year.

During the nineteenth century the Benedictine monks at Solesmes, France, revived interest in the Gregorian chants, generally regarded as among the noblest expressions of religious music in the world. Pope Pius X formally recognized their work. He also advocated frequent Communion by the laity and promoted early First Communion by children in parishes.

Pius XII, who was Pope from 1939 to 1958, wrote encyclicals on worship that received wide study and attention. These were on the following topics: *Mystici Corporis Christi* (*Mystical Body*), 1943; *Mediator Dei* (*Sacred Liturgy*), 1947.

Probably the most significant actions in many centuries have been those by Pius XII, 1955–1958, and by the Second Vatican Council, 1962–1965.

Important changes in the rites during Holy Week were decreed by Pius XII in 1955, effective in 1956. These were then called "the most far-reaching liturgical reforms in-

stituted by the Roman Catholic Church in modern times."
The changes were designed to add beauty and solemnity
to Holy Week observances and to give encouragement to
the laity to participate. The holding of certain services in
afternoon and evening hours enabled persons occupied
during working hours to attend. On Good Friday, during
the adoration of the cross, worshipers now may file forward and kiss the cross, whereas formerly they watched
the ceremony from the pews. On Holy Saturday a new
ritual enables everyone present to light a candle in a dark-
ened church. On Holy Thursday, the ancient ritual of
washing the Apostles' feet may be held; in this the priest
washes the feet of twelve men chosen from among those
worshiping. On Good Friday, all the clergy and all the
laity may now receive the Holy Communion.

By actions of 1953 and 1957 the celebration of Evening
Mass, i.e., after 4:00 P.M., was authorized, thus modifying
earlier regulations regarding the receipt of Communion
fasting. This change, again, was made to enable more persons to attend Mass and receive the Holy Communion.

The Dialogue Mass was instituted in 1958. This was
the first change in centuries in the method of participation
by the laity. In this Mass, the members make the responses
to the priest celebrating; the priest reads the Epistle and
the Gospel in Latin, and a lector reads them in the
vernacular.

After much discussion among Catholics throughout the
world, the Second Vatican Council, 1962–1965, voted in
favor of new measures, approved by Pope Paul VI, to
adapt the liturgy to the needs of the people. They authorized procedures whereby conferences of bishops in nations
and territories may use the vernacular in most parts of
the Mass and in the administration of the sacraments.

In the United States the bishops responded promptly.
They submitted translations in English of portions of the

Mass and of the ceremonies of the sacraments, for approval of the Pope. The use of the changed text began late in 1964. Throughout the world, implementation of the authorization is expected to take place slowly over a period of years.

A new provision, noted above, that a sermon is obligatory at all Masses of Sundays and holydays, went into effect in 1964.

Roman Catholic bishops have been granted discretionary authority to permit the faithful to attend Mass on Saturday instead of Sunday for special valid reasons, the Vatican's Congregation of the Council, which regulates religious observances, announced in 1964. Extensive air travel by many persons was cited as one of the reasons for authorizing the change.

A Commission on Liturgical Reforms was appointed by Pope Paul VI in 1964. This body of forty-two churchmen from twenty-six nations will supervise the enactment of changes authorized by the Vatican Council and approved by the Pope.

4

The Laity
and Their Organizations

"It is becoming old hat to talk about the need for lay people taking an active part in the church," because every octogenarian priest and bishop says the church needs more dedicated lay people. "There should be fewer generalizations about urgency and more specifics about implementation." These were conclusions of a Catholic priest, Dennis J. Geaney, O.S.A., in an article, "New Frontiers for the Laity." [1] "The mere increment of appeals without concrete implementation may produce diminishing results," he further observed.

There are laity and laity in the Roman Catholic Church, as one would expect in any large religious body. There are lay orders whose members spend much of the day in devout prayer. There are lay people who give themselves to the labor movement and work for minimum wages and a short working week. There are laymen who are distinguished scholars; there are laity who will not know for a generation or so what good Pope John was talking about when he was Pontiff from 1958 to 1963. There are laymen who campaign blindly against the United Nations, and others who are as devoted to it as was Pope John. There are laymen who think that every Fordham (Catholic) University graduate is a loyal patriotic American—and that Fordham graduates should be on the staff of the FBI to investigate the patriotism of Harvard graduates. There are laymen who work for an "open church," and those who prefer a sort of closed corporation for a church. There are Catholic people among the members of the ultraconservative John Birch Society. And a group of Catholic laymen, who edit a journal of public affairs, literature and the arts, have published several editorials saying that the atheist can be as good a citizen as the religious person. These varieties of experience indicate at least that there is broad discussion of the roles of the laity in the church, and that the laity are in many instances taking part.

In a church with a well-defined priesthood, the role of the lay person is always more limited than in the more informal bodies. Of some of the latter it is said that they are still considering the role of the pastor, thus the role of the layman is a matter of broad conjecture and of considerable freedom. In the Roman Catholic Church a layman may not administer the sacraments, *except* that of Baptism in emergency when no priest is present and a person to be baptized is believed to be in danger of or near death. The now famous Dionne quintuplets of Canada were baptized by the Roman Catholic physician who at the time was not sure how many of them would survive. Lay people are consulted in the management of parish affairs. They engage in many activities under church auspices, as noted below. And they are looking to their Church in considerable numbers in a mood of inquiry concerning their rights and duties. Probably in increasing numbers in the United States they believe that their rights and duties are not fixed forever, and that there may indeed be "new frontiers." The liturgical movements and the interest in the Bible, already referred to, are evidences of stirrings among lay people.

Historic Initiatives of Laity

Lay initiative is not something new in the history of the Catholic Church. In Assisi, Italy, the first little group of Franciscans were laymen. St. Francis of Assisi was a layman when he founded his order. With considerable hesitation his order was accepted by his Church. The first monastic movement was led by Benedict, not a priest. St. Ignatius Loyola wrote his well-known Spiritual Exercises when not ordained. The zeal of a lay person, Pauline Jaricot, is said to have had great influence in founding the Society for the Propagation of the Faith, which has greatly extended programs of foreign missions. A French layman, Frederic Ozanam, founded the Society of St. Vincent de Paul, now widely organized to give volunteer service to the sick and the poor.

To carry on their work within the Church, the laity, no matter how influential, must secure approval, confirmation, and direction from the ecclesiastical authorities, who have the main responsibility for worship, government, and the nature of teaching done in the name of the Church. Yet lay persons are not mere spectators. They "assist" at the Mass. They may now read the Scripture during the Mass. They witness to the teaching of the Church, and are to some extent employed in the vast educational enterprise (see Chapter 7, "Education"). In special cases, they may teach in theological seminaries. And the Church is a community of priesthood and laity. Neither is inferior when it comes to responsibility for the sanctification of the souls of persons.

Some Lay Organizations and Activities

The great reliance of the Church on orders for education, health, and social services, has already been noted in Chapter 1, "General Characteristics of the Roman Catholic Church." A number of lay organizations will now be described.

CATHOLIC ACTION

Pope Pius XI, who was pontiff from 1922 to 1939, defined Catholic Action as a lay apostolate with responsibility for developing in the parishes liturgical revival, youth organization, and programs on behalf of the masses of industrial workers in the cities of the world. However, the Pope named no specific activities or forms of organization and declared that these would vary from nation to nation. He specifically labeled it a religious activity. Pius XII continued to stress participation of the laity in the liturgy. During his tenure a Permanent Committee for International Congresses of the Laity was established in Rome in 1952.

National responsibility for encouraging the lay apostolate of Catholic Action in the United States is lodged in the National Council of Catholic Men and the National Council of Catholic Women, both agencies of the National Catholic Welfare Conference, Washington. Both these Councils are voluntary federations of local organizations. A major emphasis of the Council of Catholic Men is on communication. (See Chapter 5, "Communication.") It has sponsored a Catholic Hour on radio since 1930, and in recent years has arranged numerous TV programs. It distributes films. It publishes numerous pamphlets that sum up Catholic beliefs and principles.

The National Council of Catholic Women emphasizes family life, social action, international cooperation. It raises money for the Church's large foreign relief program.

CATHOLIC SOCIAL ACTION

Catholic social action is one phase of Catholic Action. The Social Action Department of the National Catholic Welfare Conference has carried on a number of specific activities. Its functions are mainly educational, with an emphasis on encouraging social action in industrial (labor-management) relations, family life, rural life, social welfare, and international relations. It has stimulated publication and discussion of the social teachings of the Church, particularly of the emphases in the social encyclicals of the Church. It has sought to apply the Papal teachings to situations in the United States.

A Committee on Parish Credit Unions of the National Catholic Welfare Conference stimulated the formation of credit unions of which there are 1,350 within parishes of the United States. Credit unions are chartered by states or by the Federal Bureau of Credit Unions. They are co-operative banks which receive deposits from and make short-term loans to their members. Credit unions may only be formed among groups of persons that associate with one another, such as the teachers of a city school system, the employees of one factory, etc., including the members of local churches. Credit unions may be small or large. Those in Catholic parishes are of all sizes. One parish credit union in Detroit assembled deposits of $135,000 and made short-term loans totaling over $1,000,000 in seven years. It also helped to organize two other credit unions.

YOUTH

The National Council of Catholic Youth, a unit of NCWC, promotes organizations of youth both in dioceses and in the colleges. It trains youth groups to work on problems by methods approved by the leaders of Catholic action. It gathers information and gives advice on youth activities and problems. In the Council are also the National Federation of Newman Clubs in colleges and universities and the National Federation of Catholic College Students.

The Catholic Youth Organization, formed first by Bishop Bernard Sheil in Chicago, has now a National Federation related to the National Council of Catholic Youth. It has both teen-age and young adult sections for youth not in colleges. Their local programs include recreation, education, social and religious activities.

In many Catholic parishes there are also Boy Scouts,

Girl Scouts, Camp Fire Girls, and junior divisions of such adult fellowships as the Knights of Columbus and the Catholic Daughters of America.

INTERRACIAL JUSTICE

There are some sixty local councils of interracial justice, related to the National Catholic Conference for Interracial Justice, Chicago. The National Council was set up in 1960, but one in New York was started in 1934. These Councils emphasize the universal teaching of the Church with respect to the dignity of persons of all races, strive to improve relations between the races, and work for equal justice for all races. The Catholic Conference was one of the organizations cooperating with the various civil-rights and religious organizations that arranged the 1963 March on Washington on behalf of national civil-rights legislation.

A lively organization of both rural clergy and lay people (mainly farmers) is the National Catholic Rural Life Conference, Des Moines. People living on farms are now fewer than 10 percent of all the population, and surely fewer than 10 percent of the farmers are Roman Catholics. The Catholic Church generally urged its immigrant families to stay in the cities where there was organized parish life. But considerable numbers of immigrants from Germany, for example, made their way to Wisconsin, Minnesota, Kansas, the Dakotas, and other states nearby, to live on farms. The NCRLC holds a well-attended annual convention, which probably passes as many resolutions as any religious organization. It urges farmers to organize credit unions (see above) and other cooperatives of all types. It favors the family farm and various forms of legislation in aid of farm people. It encourages rural parishes to make special observance of the Rogation Days in the Church year. (Rogation Sunday is the fifth Sunday after Easter;

it is also called Rural Life Sunday in other religious bodies.) The Conference holds that the relation of man to the land is one of the most fundamental of all relationships. It states that a healthy agrarianism is an essential ingredient in modern society, which becomes increasingly urban. The Conference also encourages part-time farming, where a family lives on a small farm but a member of the family also has income from another vocation. This is called "one foot on the land."

FAMILY LIFE

The Christian Family Movement, Chicago, brings together married couples for regular meetings with the purpose of devoting family life to Christ and creating communities in which Christian living is encouraged. The members are instructed to study and to act. They study the Gospels and the liturgy of the Church. Small groups meet in parishes under the guidance of priests as chaplains.

The Cana Conference Movement begun in New York is now related to the Family Life Bureau of the NCWC, Washington. Conferences for married couples are held in about 125 dioceses. Consideration is given to relations of husband and wife, parents and children, God and the family, the family and society. Most conferences are open to non-Catholic couples. In some dioceses small groups called Cana Clubs are organized as a result of the conferences. They are made up of no more than six couples in each unit.

The Family Life Bureau of NCWC, in addition to sponsoring Cana Conferences, also promotes educational programs of preparation for marriage, organization of family clubs, marriage counseling, and activities to reach large audiences through mass communications.

INDUSTRY AND TRADE

Among organizations are: The Association of Catholic Trade Unionists, New York, which conducts labor schools and forums on labor issues.

National Conference of Christian Employers and Managers, Chicago. This is as yet a relatively small organization, compared with larger and older groups in Europe, which are federated in an international organization. They bring persons together to consider the standards of Catholic teachings in the light of their situations.

Catholic Institute of the Food Industry, New York, operates only in this metropolitan area, works for high standards of practice and supports general Catholic programs.

LAY THEOLOGY INSTITUTE

An Institute of Lay Theology has been begun in San Francisco. It trains qualified Catholic laymen to work full time for salary in parishes as directors of inquiry forums and as leaders in efforts to secure converts. To be eligible for training, a man must be at least 28 years of age and a college graduate. He must enter with his military service completed. Married men are preferred. In 1963, 36 graduates of the Institute's intensive course of 10 months were working in 68 parishes in 8 Western dioceses.

Lay Appraisal of the Laity

Reviewing lay participation in the Church, Daniel Callahan, an associate editor of *The Commonweal*, says the American Catholic Church and the laity have been emerging since 1917 from the mood of the ghetto in which the Church had lived so long. The American laity are also asking persistently for fuller participation in the life and work of the Church and more opportunity to witness for the Church in society.

He asks for more genuine clergy-lay cooperation, authentic dialogues between them, development of the Church as a community in a deeper sense than now is evident, a Church willing to work in society for the welfare of others not in the Church—in short a mature laity.

"Regrettably," Mr. Callahan generalizes, "a lack of freedom in some non-theological and non-moral areas of the Church is recognized to be a major handicap to the development of the kind of layman the Church now needs in order to make its voice heard in the world. . . .

"He [the layman] is asked to be a prophetic voice in society—but he may well be courting trouble if he tries to raise such a voice within the Church. . . .

"The great difficulty . . . is not the divinely ordained authority of the Church in matters of faith and morals. Rarely does this pose a genuine problem for the layman. The real difficulty is *authoritarianism* [italics mine]: that cluster of inclinations, concepts and attitudes which is fearful of individual freedom, reliant upon the force of law and coercion to sustain belief; and convinced that the only discipline of any value is that imposed by others. It would be false to imply that the authoritarian spirit reigns supreme in the Church, especially in America. The layman does, in fact, have open to him many options and can exercise considerable freedom. For all that, the impulse among Catholic churchmen toward freedom seems weaker than toward authoritarianism." [2]

"Despite all the fine romantic statements about women's place being on a pedestal, the roots of our tradition require that women be given a 'separate' treatment because they are *not* equal, because they are inferior," observes Rosemary Lauer, associate professor at St. John's University in New York.[3] Miss Lauer was writing not only about the Catholic Church but also Western tradition in general. In Catholic schools and colleges, she states, the words of St. Thomas Aquinas, "woman exists for the man, not man for the woman," are taught. Genesis, Paul's epistles, and custom also combine to convey the impression that women are inferior.

The fact that it has never been done, writes Miss Lauer further, is not "a sufficient argument against ordaining women to the Catholic priesthood." It is not taught that the soul of a woman differs from that of a man. Pope John XXIII, she notes, wrote in his now celebrated encyclical, *Pacem in Terris* (*Peace on Earth*), in 1963: "It is obvious to everyone that women are now taking a part in public life. This is happening more rapidly, perhaps, in nations of Christian civilization, and more slowly but broadly, among peoples who have inherited other traditions or cultures. Since women are becoming ever more conscious of their human dignity, they will not tolerate being treated as mere material instruments, but demand rights befitting a human person both in domestic and in public life. . . . Human beings have the right to choose freely the state of life which they prefer, and therefore the right to set up a family with equal rights and duties for man and woman."

Second Vatican Council on the Laity

"Let pastors respectfully acknowledge that just freedom which belongs to everyone," said the Second Vatican Council in a chapter on the Laity, which in 1964 became part of the Constitution on the Church, approved by decree of the Pope. The Council specifically reminded the Church that it consists of both laity and clergy. The grace of God is freely given to people of every rank. All may contribute to the renewal of the Church. Pastors are instructed by the Council to encourage lay people to initiate activities on their own responsibility. (See Chapter 14, "Second Vatican Council.")

5

Communication

The various arts and media of communication have received considerable attention from Roman Catholic officials and agencies. This has been especially true of "mass communication" in the United States. The Church maintains a highly developed press. It arranges national and local radio and TV programs. Its scholars write numerous books and pamphlets. There is a long list of "publishers of Catholic books." There are "Catholic book clubs." There is a "Catholic Theater Conference."

Some Official Catholic Policies and Programs

There are "Church laws" and specific programs of Church organization with respect to literature and motion pictures in which there is a high degree of public interest. A few will be noted here.

The Catholic Church acts in these matters for the specific purpose of protecting the morals and the faith of its members and to aid in the salvation of souls.

With respect to books, the Church prohibits the circulation of certain works proscribed by the Holy Office. A book that is forbidden by this Office of the Holy See is forbidden throughout the world. The Church also requires the examination and approval of certain types of books prior to publication.

Proper ecclesiastical authority (i.e., ordinarily the bishop of a diocese and an officer of a religious order if the writer is a member of an order) must examine five types of books as follows: The Scriptures and annotations and commentaries thereon; books on theology, Church history, Canon Law, ethics; prayer books and related devotional materials; books on "sacred images"; and any other writings on religion and morals. A proposed book that contains no material contrary to faith and morals may be printed with an *Imprimatur* containing the words *Nihil Obstat*. *Imprimatur* means the work may be printed, and *Nihil Obstat* means "nothing stands in the way." This does not mean that the censor of books agrees with every thought, thesis, or sentence; it does mean that he finds that the work is not contrary to Catholic faith and morals.

The Holy Office "forbids" the reading of many types of books (a list known as the Index) because of content or because they have not had proper ecclesiastical approval. These include: translations or publications of Scripture by non-Catholics; writings defending heresies or attacking morals and religion; books by non-Catholics on religion that contain material contrary to the Catholic faith; books on obscene or impure topics; liturgies that change text approved by the Holy See; printed images of sacred figures not in accord with general Church law. The penalty is excommunication of publisher and author. A member of the Church may, however, request permission to read a book on the Index by writing a letter to the bishop of a diocese and stating the reason for the reading. This whole procedure has been declared "outmoded" by certain cardinals and theologians, and it has been discussed in the Second Vatican Council. Some Catholic authors are of the opinion that it would only be fair and just to grant a Catholic author a hearing if his work is under discussion, a method so far not used by the Holy Office.

The National Legion of Decency was established in

1934 by the bishops of the United States, in response to wide public condemnation of prevalent emphases in motion pictures in the nation. The bishops requested in 1938 that the following pledge be taken by all persons attending Masses in all churches and chapels of the nation on the Sunday falling after the Feast of the Immaculate Conception, which is December 8:

"In the name of the Father and of the Son and of the Holy Spirit, Amen.

"I condemn indecent and immoral motion pictures, and those which glorify crime and criminals.

"I promise to do all that I can to strengthen public opinion against the production of indecent and immoral films, and to unite with all who protest against them.

"I acknowledge my obligation to form a right conscience about pictures that are dangerous to my moral life. As a member of the Legion of Decency, I pledge myself to remain away from them. I promise, further, to stay away altogether from places of amusement which show them as a matter of policy."

The National Legion of Decency continuously evaluates commercial motion pictures and issues ratings for the guidance of Catholics. When it approves films it also indicates whether they are endorsed for adults only, and designates certain ones for children.

The National Office for Decent Literature was set up by the bishops in 1938 particularly to oppose the circulation to young people of indecent periodicals, books (especially the comics), and pamphlets. The NODL wishes to safeguard the idealism of youth by efforts to remove objectionable titles from circulation and sale, by encouraging the publication of "good literature," by developing "worth-while reading habits." The NODL offers to organizations and individuals lists containing its evaluations of current literature. A code adopted in 1956 labels as objectionable publications, among others, those that glorify crime, encourage disrespect for law, portray sex facts "offensively," feature lewd illustrations, are "blasphemous," and hold up to ridicule any race or religion. The great zeal of some local groups interested in NODL, which at times include both Catholics and others, has received both approval and disapproval from the American public. Disapproval has come from some Catholics as well as others, when it appears that local groups have taken "extra-legal" means (including boycotts) to remove titles from the shelves of vendors, or have regarded themselves as "special assistants" of a police force or of a district attorney. The advice of NODL to members of the Catholic Church has been fully respected as appropriate by non-Catholics and Catholics.

Newspapers and Magazines

The Catholic Press Association reported in 1964, 131 "newspapers" with a total circulation of over 5,500,000. The Association uses the word newspaper differently, however, from that of the general public, which thinks of a newspaper as a daily publication. The Catholic newspapers include 72 weeklies, published locally; 44 weekly diocesan editions of national newspapers; 2 national newspapers; and 9 foreign language newspapers.

There were, according to the Association, 105 magazines accepting advertising, and 209 magazines not taking advertising, a total of 374 magazines. These had a circulation of about 21,500,000.

Thus there were 505 newspapers and magazines with a combined circulation of over 27,000,000. Special directories were not included.

The National Catholic Welfare Conference News Service

NCWC News Service issues much material to many of the Catholic newspapers and periodicals. It provides news, editorial matter, feature articles, and photographs. Its services are also available to radio and TV stations and to communication media in other countries. This service is used at the discretion of the editors. The non-Catholic reader may wish to be informed that the editors are not required to duplicate material from NCWC News Service. A reader of a number of Catholic periodicals will be at once impressed by the diversities as well as by the unities.

Among national periodicals well-known in Catholic and other circles are: *America,* New York, a weekly review edited by the Jesuit Fathers; *The Commonweal,* New York, a weekly journal of public affairs, literature, and the arts, edited by laymen, which now has a regular Protestant columnist.

Diocesan papers of the larger dioceses that frequently receive public attention are *The Criterion,* Indianapolis; *The Pilot,* Boston; and *The Catholic News,* New York.

Among special periodicals one may note *The Pope Speaks,* Washington, which publishes addresses and other communications of the Popes; and *The Catholic Worker,* New York, a pacifist monthly, edited by a lay group, concerning which it has been said that the Catholic Church does not know what to do with it or what it would do without it.

National newspapers include *Our Sunday Visitor* with 12 separate editions; *The Register* with 32 diocesan editions; and *The National Catholic Reporter,* Kansas City, Mo.

Particularly since the ecumenical outreach of Pope John XXIII, during his reign, 1958–1963, observers note in the Catholic press of the United States increasing attention to news and developments among Eastern Orthodox and Protestant bodies.

Books

"I can understand the popularity of a Cardinal Cushing, because many Americans notice high officials, but how can I explain Thomas Merton?" This question came from a British visitor who periodically comes to the United States. For Thomas Merton since 1944 has published some thirty books dealing mainly with the "interior life" of man. He deals with mysticism and contemplation. He is read eagerly by non-Catholics as well as by his coreligionists. He entered the Trappist Monastery at Gethsemani, Kentucky, in 1941; was ordained a priest in 1949; is presently Master of Novices at the monastery. This popular author is a member of the Order of Cistercians of the Strict Observance.

The spiritual struggles and meditations recorded by Thomas Merton are but one facet of a wide range of Catholic literature, much of it recorded in books. Some 1,050 "Catholic books" and 200 "Catholic pamphlets" were published in 1962, according to a compilation made by Eugene F. Williging, director of the libraries of the Catholic University, Washington, in 1963. Some 115 publishers produced Catholic books, this figure including both the distinctly Catholic book houses, and the several Catholic departments, some large, of general commercial firms. The recent books classified as Catholic may be arranged under such headings as Art, the Bible, Biography, Prayer and the Devotional Life, Church and State, Civil Rights, Drama, Doctrine, Ecumenical, Education, Fiction, History, Juvenile, Liturgy, Missions, Philosophy, Poetry, Psychology, Social Science, Vatican Council, Reference Works.

Books of "ready reference" generally in use include *The National Catholic Almanac*, an annual, edited by Father Felician A. Foy, published by St. Anthony's Guild Press, Paterson, N.J.; and the *Official Catholic Directory*, edited by Thomas B. Kenedy, published yearly by P. J. Kenedy and Sons, New York. The first of these includes numerous details on most aspects of Catholic life and work; the second lists every parish, the county in which it is located, the name and street address of all priests in charge of parishes, and much pertinent information on colleges, and other Catholic institutions.

There are ten Catholic book clubs, one of these specializing in books for youth, and another in works for children.

Radio and Television

Among the recent radio and TV programs produced by or in cooperation with Catholic agencies, some of the widely known are those of the National Council of Catholic Men, affiliated with the National Catholic Welfare Conference, Washington. The radio work began in the 1920's; the TV productions, in 1953. Its "Catholic Hour" on radio is broadcast over a large hookup. "The Catholic Hour" on TV is available on all Sundays in January, May, August, and October. During other months programs are televised by Protestant and Jewish agencies under a "tri-faith" arrangement.

"Christian in Action" has been another regular Sunday radio program of NCCM. It has included news, an editorial by a Catholic editor, and a question box period.

"The Church of the Air" has been a tri-faith radio program, in which NCCM cooperates by furnishing a program on one Sunday of each month.

Other tri-faith TV programs in which NCCM shares

time are series named "Look Up and Live" and "Lamp Unto My Feet."

Special Easter and Christmas programs are arranged.

Other well-known radio programs are "The Sacred Heart Program" of the Jesuit Fathers (also on TV); "The Ave Maria Hour" of the Graymoor Friars on behalf of St. Christopher's Inn; the discussions of the Christophers; "The Hour of St. Francis," by the Third Order of St. Francis (also on TV).

Local TV stations frequently televise a Mass or a special Catholic service.

The Theater

The National Catholic Theater Conference meets every two years, bringing together priests, teachers, and students with common interests in drama. It is a national association with an office in Washington, D.C. The Department of Speech and Drama of the Catholic University, Washington, offers numerous courses, maintains a University Theater, and organizes a company of touring National Players. The Blackfriars' Guild, New York, reported to be the "oldest off-Broadway" theater, emphasizes experimental plays.

For the welfare of Catholic persons in the theater, the Catholic Actors Guild of America, New York, offers numerous services. An Actor's Chapel is maintained by St. Malachy's Church, New York.

Texts of plays are published by The Catholic Dramatic Guild and the Catholic Dramatic Movement, both with offices in Milwaukee.

The Second Vatican Council adopted a "schema" or agenda on "Instruments of Social Communication," which is summarized in Chapter 14, "Second Vatican Council."

6

Population Problems
and Family Responsibility

"The problem, everyone talks of it, is that of . . . population increases on the one hand, and family morality on the other," said Pope Paul VI in the course of "remarks" in Rome to a group of cardinals in June, 1964. The Pope went on: "It is an extremely grave problem. It touches on the mainsprings of human life. It touches on the feelings and interests most close to the experience of men and women. It is an extremely complex and delicate problem. The Church recognizes the multiple aspects of it . . . , that of married people, that of their freedom, of their conscience, of their love, of their duty. . . .

"But the Church must also affirm . . . God's law, by her interpreted, taught, favored, and defended. And the Church will have to proclaim this law of God in the light of scientific, social, and psychological truths which in these times have undergone new and ample study and documentation. . . .

"The question is being subjected to study, as wide and profound as possible, as grave and honest as it must be, on a subject of such importance." Meanwhile, present norms are binding, and "no one in the Church should issue pronouncements contrary to those norms." [1]

Marriage Laws and Norms

Among the marriage laws and norms of the Roman Catholic Church are these:

The primary purpose or end of marriage is the generation of children and their education. Secondary, are the encouragement of mutual love and aid, support of a common life, and satisfaction of normal wishes and desires. Further, the union in marriage is permanent, and can be broken only by death. The marriage laws of the Church are binding upon all who are validly baptized. Catholics may, on securing ecclesiastical permission, marry baptized or unbaptized non-Catholics, in the presence of a duly ordained priest. These non-Catholics, however, become subject to the marriage laws of the Church.

A considerable number of impediments to marriage are recognized, including age (under age 14 for a female, under 16 for a male); a vow of perpetual chastity for the purpose of entering a religious order; impotence; existence of a previous marriage; the obligation of ordination to the priesthood; close blood relationships; a defect in consent; presence of a situation opposed to the nature of marriage.

Decrees of nullity are in rare instances granted by ecclesiastical courts. The Sacred Tribunal of the Rota in the Vatican is a court of final appeal. The Rota reports on marriage cases only ten years after decisions. It has reported that in the year 1952 it had given rulings in 188 cases from all parts of the world. Separations are also at times permitted by the ecclesiastical authorities.

The Churches of the Eastern Rite, Roman Catholic, have marriage laws differing in only a few respects from those of the Latin or Western Rite. Both agree that in a marriage between a person of the Latin Rite and one of the Eastern, the rite of the groom is used, and children born of the marriage shall be baptized in that rite.

FAMILY LIMITATION

Family limitation is given approval as moral only if by: (1) delay in entering upon a marriage; (2) prolonged abstinence after marriage by mutual consent; and (3) periodic continence, or as it is generally known, the rhythm method, also by mutual consent. By the last method an estimate is made of the days when a woman is probably infertile in the cycle of menstruation, and intercourse is had only on those days. The days are determined not only by the calendar but also by basal body temperature. The Church is encouraging research fully to test the rhythm method. It is defended by some physicians who contend it is as reliable as the use of contraceptives, including the recently developed chemical compounds taken orally as tablets or pills. The Church condemns as immoral procedures both abortion and sterilization. Drugs may not be taken for a directly contraceptive intention. (For discussion of marriage by the Vatican Council see Chapter 14, "Second Vatican Council.")

THERAPEUTIC ABORTION

On therapeutic abortion (that is, a medical procedure to save a mother's life or protect her from serious illness) Pope Pius XI wrote in the encyclical, *Casti Connubii* (*On Christian Marriage*), 1930: "However much we may pity the mother whose health and even life is gravely imperiled in the performance of the duty allotted to her by nature, nevertheless what could be sufficient reason for excusing in any way the direct murder of the innocent? This is precisely what we are dealing with here. Whether inflicted upon mother or upon child, it is against the precept of God and the law of nature: 'Thou shalt not kill.' The life of each is equally sacred, and no one has the power, nor even the public authority to destroy it." This is a position strongly opposed by many non-Catholics. However, the Catholic position has apparently not been implemented by advocating legislation on the subject in the United

States, possibly because medical technology has proceeded to such an extent that physicians are probably seldom faced with the terrible dilemma involved. It seems to be usually possible to induce an indirect abortion, with the purpose of removing diseased tissue or condition in the mother, thus indirectly causing the death of the fetus.

DIVORCE

All religious bodies seem to agree that the frequency of divorce is one of the serious social problems. Many non-Catholics go further and say that the current state of divorce laws and legal procedures related thereto are inadequate, even deplorable, and that the present situation calls urgently for remedies. But Catholics and most non-Catholics seem to divide in opinion regarding the ways and means of improvement. Many non-Catholics favor liberalizing divorce laws by generally allowing such grounds as cruelty and desertion where state laws do not provide such provisions. The general Catholic position is to oppose liberalization of the divorce laws, and in some states the Church has even opposed study of divorce problems by legislative committees.

MIXED MARRIAGES

On the matter of mixed marriages, that is, between Roman Catholics and those of other faiths, the Roman Catholic position is far different from that of most religious bodies and of the community at large. The Roman Catholic Church officially discourages mixed marriages, but many of these are contracted every year. The Church permits them only under strict conditions: a Catholic priest must officiate; the Catholic party shall be placed in no danger of being converted to a non-Catholic religion; the Catholic member shall strive to convert the non-Catholic to Catholicism; and both parties must promise in advance that children shall be brought up in the Catholic faith. Probably most non-Catholics believe the Church's position to be intransigent or intolerant. (See Chapter 14, "Second Vatican Council.")

At the 1963 session of the Second Vatican Council, changes in the Church's position on mixed marriages were requested by Joseph Cardinal Frings of Cologne, West Germany, and Right Reverend Hilaire Capucci, Superior General of the Order of St. Basil, Syria. Cardinal Frings urged his Church to declare the validity of mixed marriages contracted in the presence of a non-Catholic minister, and that ecclesiastical penalties for such marriages should be removed. He said that such a step would help to create a better atmosphere between the Catholic Church and other bodies and to prepare the way for more fruitful ecumenical activity. He also thought that the Church should continue to express general disapproval of mixed marriages. The Superior General, Capucci, agreed with the Cardinal. Both spoke on a draft of a proposed statement of the Church on Ecumenism, or the movement for cooperation and unity among churches.

ADOPTION

Public policies of adoption of children in strict accord with religious heritage of children is favored by Roman Catholics, a practice that has raised opposition among other churches and in the community at large. It has often been a force making for division among churches.

Wide Public Discussion

There has been wide public discussion of the Church's positions, but especially that on birth control. There are probably two main reasons: the population explosion, so-called, along with hunger in the world and the inability of many nations to keep the gains in food production up with population gains; much evidence that many Catholic women use contraceptives.

As for the first, population pressure on food supply, this is surely not wholly a Catholic problem. Many of the nations or areas with this problem do not have large Catholic memberships, e.g., India, Japan, and South East Asia. It is largely a Catholic problem in Latin America, where recent reports show the world's highest population gains.

That Catholic women in large numbers use contraceptives may now be put into the category of common knowledge in the United States. But, it is understood, that when they inform a priest of their practice they are denied the sacraments of the Church. When many choose to continue the practice without access to the sacraments, this creates a most significant issue of churchmanship.

A Catholic mother writes an article, "Why I Believe in Birth Control," appearing first in *Jubilee*, a Catholic journal, then in the *Saturday Evening Post* and in the *Reader's Digest*. She says that her Church puts married Catholics into an "impossible situation." She pleads that the matter be left to private conscience. The rhythm method, which she has tried to follow, is so unsure that practice of it results in tension and removes joy from marriage.

At about the same time Bishop John J. Wright of Pittsburgh said before the National Convention of the Family Life Bureau of the NCWC, that the United States is a "contraceptive civilization," contrary to Christianity.

In England, the Catholic bishops united in a statement in 1964 condemning "the pill" used as a contraceptive. A priest was then quoted as saying that surely a distinction must be made between a drug and the other forms of contraception. The British bishops said approval might later be given to a drug that would aid in making the cycle of menstruation regular. In one newsletter a Catholic official said that Church laws had undergone immense changes over the centuries, and it was not certain that the present Catholic attitude toward contraception would not change.

The Commonweal, New York, a weekly review of public affairs, literature, and the arts, edited by Catholic laymen, ran a symposium in a special issue, June 5, 1964, on "Responsible Parenthood." The editors wrote that the "issue of responsible parenthood has become a crucial one for the contemporary Church. In part, history has brought this about. The world in which the Church now exists is not the same world which existed a century ago. Not only has the social character of life changed radically, but along with that change has come a marked shift in the moral consensus among non-Catholics. Though less dramatic, the Catholic moral consensus has also undergone a shift. No longer is the idea of birth limitation rejected out of hand." A "wide range of perspectives" was presented in the issue.

A priest reported in this symposium that he began to modify his adjectives in sermons on birth control when a member informed him that his wife had borne "nine tiny monstrosities in a row," and after another said his wife had presented him with five sets of twins in as many years. The Catholic layman, the priest went on, is properly told that Catholic teaching is based on "the natural law," but the layman also knows that this law is formulated by human beings. Might there not be new applications, new interpretations, in the light of new situations?

A Catholic physician, John C. Rock, wrote in his book, *The Time Has Come,*[2] that "the pill" might properly be used to control fertility, and that there might, after a time, be a change in his Church's position. Richard Cardinal Cushing of Boston, in whose archdiocese Dr. Rock resides, promptly stated that the physician did not speak for the Church, and that the book was not free of doctrinal error.

7

Education

"Parents are bound by a most grave obligation to provide to the best of their ability for the religious and moral, as well as for the physical and civil, education of their children, and for their temporal well-being." Thus reads Canon Law. Further: "Catholic children must not attend non-Catholic, neutral or mixed schools." Only the bishop may decide under what circumstances, "attendance at such schools may be tolerated without danger of perversion to the pupils." The Plenary Council of the Catholic Bishops held at Baltimore, 1884, provided that a parochial school shall be established "near every church." In actual practice, many (perhaps half) of the children of Catholic parents attend public and non-Catholic private schools. In 1965 the *Official Catholic Directory* reported 1,304,328 public-high-school pupils and 3,295,899 public elementary-school pupils receiving religious instruction in their parishes. Probably a considerable number of Catholic children do not or cannot receive religious instruction, although every parish is required to offer it to public-school pupils.

Discussion of issues and contemplated changes are numerous. The Church finds it difficult adequately to finance modern elementary and secondary education. Some parishes use methods to raise money to maintain parochial schools that are subject to much public criticism—e.g., bingo games. (In other dioceses the playing of bingo is prohibited in the parishes by order of bishops.)

80

"Shared time" or dual enrollment has been advocated, and some experiments are under way. Under this arrangement, the pupils of parochial schools receive part of their instruction in public schools, or certain grades only attend public schools.

Just as there were school issues in the early days of the nation, so they persist today. Some of the warmest have to do with the question of Federal aid for private as well as for public schools.

Evolution of the Catholic System

The earliest Christian education was that of Christ's Apostles. That of the Apostolic Church consisted of their preaching and instruction of children in preparation for Baptism and Confirmation. The purpose was to communicate knowledge of Christian truth and to inculcate the practice of religion. This was carried on by bishops and priests. A characteristic of this instruction was the combination of religious instruction with moral discipline. Soon there were also schools under bishops' supervision that prepared young men for the priesthood.

To the Catholic, the liturgy also has an educational purpose. The Mass appeals to mind as well as emotion. The various portions of the liturgy convey lessons to the participants who are expected to respond through thought and feelings. The liturgical year (see Chapter 3, "Liturgical Movements") with its varied emphases is also educational in effect.

As the Church spread from the Mediterranean area to the north of Europe, missionaries were teachers as well as preachers. The Church carried the teachings of Christianity along with elements of classical literature and culture. In the Middle Ages the Church cooperated with civil rulers in organizing parochial schools for the education of children. The early curricula were quite simple: religion and a few other subjects. But they were adapted to the needs of people emerging from primitive tribal life and they laid a basis for the much more systematic education that came later.

The monasteries of the Benedictine Order became the depositories of much of the ancient learning: manuscripts were carefully preserved and copied, research was encouraged, libraries were started, and the beginnings of professional training were offered. In the monasteries of the West the Latin classics survived the holocausts of the Middle Ages. The monasteries conducted schools not only for novices of the order but also "outer" schools for lay students. Here liberal arts and music were studied along with religion. Here records were kept of the details of medieval life, which became invaluable sources for later historians. Here dignity was accorded to the beginnings of the teaching profession.

Two other developments were of importance. The philosophy of the Greeks, particularly of Aristotle, was restudied. Thomas Aquinas endeavored to use Greek thought as one means of attaining a rational basis of belief. Scholasticism, the system evolved by Catholic scholars, provided training in strict logical reasoning, and thus contributed to the development of Catholic education in general. In it the truths of revelation and the results of reasoning were harmonized. It also made use of the findings of early pagan science.

Another great contribution to education came from the orders. Some, e.g., the Institute of the Brothers of the Christian Schools and the Society of Jesus, stressed the education of Catholic youths. Orders of women devoted themselves to Christian education of girls. These aimed to combine the inculcation of religious truth with the pursuit of so-called secular knowledge. Thus arose a specific

Roman Catholic system of education, from parish elementary schools to the universities.

In the United States, this Catholic system was developed by voluntary contributions. This has meant that Catholics pay both the taxes levied on citizens for the support of public schools and also contribute toward the support of their own system.

Extent of the Catholic System

In the United States, the Roman Catholic system of education is organized in distinct types, with figures from *The Official Catholic Directory*, 1965.

Elementary schools, in which the teachers are mainly in religious orders of women. In 1965 there were 10,503 elementary parochial and institutional schools with 4,476,-881 students; also 428 elementary Catholic schools classified as "private," with 89,928 pupils.

High schools, numbering 1,566, maintained both by religious orders and by dioceses, with 698,032 students; also 899 Catholic private secondary schools, with 397,487 students.

Colleges and universities, generally conducted by religious orders, numbering 304 with 384,526 students.

Seminaries, diocesan, for training candidates for the priesthood, numbering 117 with 17,494 students; also 479 seminaries and "scholasticates" maintained by orders, with 22,230 students.

There are 9,268 "diocesan students" in other seminaries; and 141 "protective" educational institutions with 16,300 students.

The total number of students under Catholic instruction, including those in public schools receiving religious teaching, was some 10,701,373.

There were 12,346 priests teaching full time; brothers

teaching, 5,868; sisters teaching, 104,314; lay teachers, 75,103; "scholastics" teaching, 1,125; a total of 198,750 full-time teachers.

Public Funds for Private Schools

General Federal aid for education has been advocated for several decades as one means of equalizing educational opportunities and facilities, because per capita incomes in some states are lower than in others. Bills have been debated in Congress from time to time. These have provided for Federal grants-in-aid to the states for the support of public or tax-supported elementary and secondary education. However, in spite of much support from organizations of public-school teachers, organized labor, women's organizations, etc., no bill with these provisions has ever passed both Houses of Congress. Opposition has come from advocates of economy, from those fearing Federal control of hitherto state functions, and from those who have favored inclusion of private, and especially the church-related, including the parochial, schools.

Aid for parochial schools has been favored by many Roman Catholics, and opposed by many Protestants, Orthodox, and Jews. The case against it usually is stated in terms of "separation of church and state," the argument being that government aid of religious education would violate the traditional separation in the United States.

A comprehensive statement of the position of the Roman Catholic Church was made in 1955, concluding that private schools have "full right" to public aid, is here summarized:

"Private and church-related schools in America exist not by sufferance but by right." The Supreme Court's decision in the "celebrated Oregon school case" established this as a constitutional right.

The bishops note that American education in the early period of our history was entirely in private and church-related schools. From them came both the "guiding intellectual and moral impulses which led to the definition and establishment of American freedom" and the leadership of the country in the period of establishing the United States.

"The rise and vigorous expansion of the American educational system is cited, correctly, as one of the major achievements of Western civilization. . . . The plain physical fact of the school system is a matter for unanimous congratulation."

Such education in America rests on the parent's right under natural law to determine how his child should be educated as well as on "the law of the land." Catholic parents realize that the "mind of the Church," as interpreted by "their spiritual leaders, the bishops," insists upon "the positive training of their children in the fundamentals of religion," which is only possible in "schools dedicated to the purpose . . . With magnificent generosity, they have provided the indicated means, the Catholic school."

But this is no infringement on public education. "The private school provides a saving and challenging variety in the total system, beneficial to the whole and manifestly fruitful in its effects." Such schools teach both the accepted curriculum and "positive religion." In 1852 the First Plenary Council of American bishops "earnestly recommended" parochial schools. In 1884 the Third Plenary Council declared that "the school was to be a part of every well-organized parish."

Recognizing that critics are particularly vocal in their complaints of the divisiveness of the parochial schools, the bishops said: "Surely, Christianity, with its primary inculcation of love of God and love of neighbor is not divisive. Only those who teach hatred teach division; those who teach love teach unity. . . . Positive Christian training . . . provides the strongest cement that can possibly bind a nation together. . . . We are a pluralistic society that postulates not uniformity but rather unity in variety."

The bishops concluded by stating their conviction that the private and church-related schools have "full right to be considered and dealt with as components of the American educational system . . . The students of these schools have the right to benefit from those measures, grants, or aids which are manifestly designed for the health, safety and welfare of American youth, irrespective of the school attended."

In recent years private, including Roman Catholic parochial schools, have become eligible for government aid for school lunches, for the grants and loans authorized by the Defense Education Act to encourage the teaching of science and mathematics, for special Federal funds for schools in communities overwhelmed by Federal defense activities, and for the grants and loans available for construction of buildings for higher education. In a few states nonreligious textbooks are furnished to private as well as to public schools. Catholic students like all others are eligible for educational grants to veterans, and for special scholarships and fellowships in higher education. Private as well as public medical schools are also eligible for receipt of Federal grants for research and construction of buildings and laboratories. However, no Federal money may be used to construct chapels or other places for worship. The Federal Government also makes grants for the construction of hospitals, public and private, and many of these hospitals conduct schools of nursing.

Shared Time or Dual Enrollment

One way out that is being tested and discussed (and not universally favored by Catholics) is called shared time or dual school enrollment. This is an arrangement in which the school time of children is shared between a public school and a church day school. Thus students enrolled in a church day school are also enrolled in a nearby public school for part of their general education. Each system remains in control of its own facilities, curriculum, schedules, and other functions. Decisions with regard to details of the arrangement must be made carefully in advance.

There has already been a good deal of experience with the plan. In the Southfield, Michigan, Public School District, 182, parochial-school pupils are studying mathematics, science, music, shop, arts and crafts, homemaking, and physical education. In fifty local school districts of Michigan various shared-time or dual-enrollment plans are already in effect. In Philadelphia, Pennsylvania, over 110 pupils in 10th grade of parochial schools spend half their school time in public technical schools. Among other cities with experience are Pittsburgh, Pennsylvania; Hamilton, Ohio; Springfield, Illinois; St. Louis, Missouri; and St. Paul, Minnesota. Plans are being made at this writing in Chicago, Ill., the state of Oregon, and many other places.

Recognition of the financial burden of Catholic parents who pay taxes to support public schools and also contribute to the support of parochial schools led the General Board of the National Council of Churches in 1964 to adopt a policy statement favoring "further experimentation with and continuing evaluation of dual enrollment for classroom instruction as a viable provision for those who for conscience' sake, maintain separate schools."

The National Council's Policy Statement reads in part:

"Public education in the United States is for all children regardless of race, creed, color, or economic status.

"In the main, in this country, Protestants and Orthodox on the one hand and Roman Catholics on the other, have chosen to take different paths to discharge their educational responsibilities for the nurture of their children.

"While approximately one-half of the Roman Catholic children are in public school the officially approved system is one composed of parochial schools organized under the total direction of Church authorities. While some Protestant and Orthodox children are in parochial schools or church day schools—perhaps a half million—most Protestant and Orthodox children are enrolled in public schools.

"The rapidly increasing number of children and the rapidly increasing costs of education, along with other factors have caused Roman Catholic educators and parents in recent years to ask for public funds in discharging part or all of their educational responsibility. Assistance is often asked for that portion of the task most clearly identified with 'general education.' Protestant and Orthodox educators and others have generally favored the use of tax funds only for public education, and resisted the use of public funds for church-related schools.

"So far this unresolved difference has prevented direct grants to religious elementary and secondary schools; it has also hindered the passage of general legislation for federal aid to public education.

"Resistance and opposition, however, are not a satisfactory permanent stance for Christians . . .

"We know of no legal opinion holding that dual school enrollment violates the federal constitution. Most states' constitutions or educational legislation appear either to permit or not to forbid dual school enrollment. . . .

"We believe that boys and girls now limited by the resources of some religious day schools will be benefited by the equipment and program offerings for the portion of the time they attend the public school. We believe that benefits will ensue for all children if those now enrolled in separate systems have the opportunity to associate with each other through dual school enrollment. We believe that this association and intermingling of the children in the school will result in a broadened support for public education and will serve to unify our now partially divided communities. At the same time, we reaffirm our support of the system of public education in the United States of America. It provides a context in which all individuals may share in an education which contributes to the full development of their capacities. It serves as a major cohesive force in our pluralistic society. It is our hope that dual school enrollment may prove to be a means of helping our nation to maintain the values of a general system of public education, yet at the same time meeting the needs of those who desire a system of church-related education, while upholding the historic American principle of the separation and interaction of church and state."

How Much Academic Freedom?

Traditionally in Catholic institutions, dissent of student or professor has been assumed to be "error," and this has been disposed of simply on the principle that "error has no rights," Leslie Dewart of St. Michael's College, Toronto, wrote in an article, "Academic Freedom and Catholic Dissent." [1] The "unsophisticated" position summarized above is becoming "increasingly rare," thinks Professor Dewart, and is yielding to one indicating that the errant person has rights even if his error has not, and these personal rights must be respected.

"The faith does not imply immutability and fixity. On the contrary, we have recently—especially since Newman

[John Cardinal Newman, English churchman, 1801–1890] begun to realize that the Christian doctrine, because of its sociohistorical dimension, truly and fittingly develops in time." Indeed, he quotes Pius XII in his encyclical *Divino Afflante Spiritu* (*Biblical Studies*), 1943, advising that "all the children of the Church . . . avoid that somewhat indiscreet zeal which considers everything new to be for that very reason a fit subject for attack or suspicion."

Professor Dewart goes on: "To propose new ideas is an integral part of the teaching function which all the faithful of the Church share in virtue of their faith. The professional Christian scholar does so, moreover, in virtue of a special calling on his part."

"We are not members of the Church because we are subject to its government's authority: it is rather the other way round. Consequently, though we are conscience bound to obey legitimate commands, our duty to the Church is not formally discharged by our obedience to the sacred government of the Church. To live the Christian life demands much more, and even more difficult tasks, perhaps, than mere obedience: it demands initiative, spontaneity, and the engagement of human existence on its own self-creative task. . . .

"Freedom of conscience and the individual's duty to the whole Church require a 'loyal opposition,' . . .

"The Christian academy best serves the interests of the Church when it exercises *its* freedom in order to realize in a Christian way its own nature as academy, that is in order to devote itself to the cultivation of the intellect and the promotion of free inquiry. The university that does not allow freedom to all its members, has, by definition, renounced its freedom and, therefore, has abdicated its academic responsibilities to the Christian Church. . . .

"The right of the academic member to academic freedom is not his right to maintain his own individual views against everybody else's: it is his right to participate, in virtue of his duty and his accepted Christian vocation in the common task of the Christian academic group. . . .

"Academic freedom, in the last analysis, is nothing else than freedom of conscience discharged in the context of a common intellectual Christian life."

8

Charities
or Social Services

Roman Catholics speak both formally and popularly of "charities," using the word often as meaning social services, social work, or social welfare. Writes Monsignor Raymond J. Gallagher, then executive director, the National Conference of Catholic Charities: "The creed and practice of Catholicism and the exercise of charity are not merely compatible concepts. Religious practice is an externalizing of creed. Charity, or if one prefers social service, is an implementation of creed. Religion is understood in its simplest definition as a love of God by the creature, embellished by an active love of neighbor. As the affluence of our neighbor is diminished, the obligation to love is increased. It follows that Catholic charity exemplified by social service is an essential part of a Catholic's religion. Catholic social service is understood as an extension of a divine command." [1]

Early Institutions

In the early period of Catholic parishes in the cities of the United States, the needs of dependent, neglected, and handicapped persons were often met when religious orders of women started institutions for orphaned children and for the aged.

Personal service was also stressed by volunteer organizations. An example of these is the Society of St. Vincent de Paul. This was organized in France in 1833 by Frederic Ozanam. The first Society in the United States was formed in St. Louis in 1845. This Society is organized in

parish conferences of which there are some 4,600 in the
United States with a membership of about 38,000 laymen.
Their purpose is to aid members of the local churches in
the practice of Christlike works of mercy. The Vincentians
include in their local programs the encouragement of religious education, visiting prisoners, spiritual counseling,
practical aid to the sick and handicapped, emergency financial assistance. Funds are raised by personal gifts of
members and by "poor boxes" in parish churches.

From Parish to Diocesan Organization

Up to the twentieth century, Catholic welfare services
were largely local, at the parish level. Then began broader
organization in the dioceses. This was set up by appointment by the bishop of a priest trained in social work as
diocesan director of Catholic charities. He was charged
with the responsibility of coordinating the work of the
organizations and institutions in the diocese, which were
generally under religious orders of men or of women.

Now the diocesan director of charities heads a staff of
professionally trained persons. Together, they study needs
and devise ways and means of meeting them. In many
cities Catholic institutions are represented in councils of
social agencies or welfare federations. They also in many
instances participate in united funds or community chests,
which make annual appeals for funds. Where Catholic
charities do not take part in united funds, the diocesan
director has the responsibility of raising money for the
support of the welfare agencies.

Rise of Public Social Welfare

With the rise in the twentieth century of large programs
of social welfare supported by taxation and administered

by public agencies, the question of the relation of Catholic institutions to this development naturally arose. The parish and the diocesan work, in more than one sense, became less inclusive in its social services. Catholic individuals participate, like all other citizens, in such as Old Age, Survivors, and Disability Insurance (commonly called Social Security), in public Old Age Assistance for needy persons, in Public Aid to Mothers of Dependent Children, in somewhat similar programs for the blind, and other related activities. They may receive public general relief from towns and cities.

What Is the Major Catholic Emphasis?

What then is the major emphasis of Catholic charities? Monsignor Raymond J. Gallagher answers that the main attention is "focused on the dependent and neglected child." [2] This service is not altogether through institutions. "Varieties" of other services are now offered. Also, the Catholic charities have increasingly recommended "cottage-type" institutions rather than the older, larger "congregate-type" for dependent children.

Catholic officials in the United States usually further the policy of complete care of children under Catholic auspices. They do not share a view often held in social welfare circles that private organizations should chiefly demonstrate or experiment—and then turn functions over to the public agencies. They also do not subscribe to the theory that Catholic service should be given to neglected children for a time so that they can later be transferred to a state agency. They believe in offering full, regular services to children side by side with those of public institutions.

Other areas of activity are those for the aging, family service, recreation for youth, health education, and some more specialized, as for the members of the armed forces. The crises and strains of families under modern conditions have led to increasing development of family service departments in diocesan charities. These do counseling in a broad sense, supplementing that done by the parish priests in their contacts with members. One of the prominent organizations with recreation programs is the Catholic Youth Organization. (See Chapter 4, "The Laity and Their Organizations.")

Statistics in the *Official Catholic Directory,* New York, 1965, reveal the following data on social welfare institutions:

```
Orphanages and Infant Asylums ............. 257
Resident children ........................ 23,379
Children in Foster Homes ................ 23,435
Homes for the Aged ........................ 387
Guests .................................. 35,560
```

The Hospitals

From early days the Catholic Church has sponsored hospitals. In 1965, there were, according to the *Official Catholic Directory:*

```
General Hospitals ........................... 808
Bed Capacity .......................... 147,319
Patients Treated Annually ............. 16,571,588
Special Hospitals or Sanitoria ............... 144
Bed Capacity ............................ 13,741
Patients Treated Annually .............. 324,055
```

There were also 341 Catholic schools of nursing with a total enrollment of 35,430 students.

9

Religious
Liberty

A policy of "no special privilege to any [religious] group and no restriction on the religious liberty of any citizen," was declared by the Roman Catholic bishops of the United States in 1948. This has been construed by Catholics and others as a plain statement in favor of separation of church and state and of religious liberty for all.

This statement, somewhat overlooked in church circles in the United States, differed markedly from statements often heard earlier. A Protestant official once reported that a Roman Catholic priest had said: "Our position is actually such that in the name of your principles we ask for religious freedom, but if we ever have a majority in the U.S. we will, in the name of our principles, deny freedom to you."

This latter interpretation has deeply troubled many Roman Catholics in the United States, and in other nations. A rapidly increasing number of Roman Catholics have ceased to accept it. The democracy of American life has undoubtedly affected Roman Catholics and others. Catholics have found religious liberty in the United States good for their Church, and they would regard it as a gross injustice to ask for its denial to others.

Some Sources of Difficulty

A considerable number of the American people have had difficulty with respect to the Roman Catholic positions. This has been explained in part at least by the theory of American democracy that the final authority is the voice and vote of the people. This has been regarded as inconsistent with an absolutist position. The final authority of the Pope, in morals as well as religion, has led some to believe that there is at least a strong possibility of essential conflict between the political institutions of the United States and the Roman Catholic religion.

Further, the Roman Catholic Church is an international institution, with great authority assigned to its central administration located in Vatican City. By contrast, the form of government in the United States provides for separation of authority, or checks and balances, among the legislative, judicial, and executive branches; and also for division of responsibility among local, state, and national political institutions. Thus there has plainly been fear, expressed and unexpressed, that the Catholic concentration of authority in morals unduly influences the action of Catholic citizens in social, economic, and public policy.

But the overt behavior of Catholic citizens in actual situations has demonstrated clearly their steadfast adherence to American political democracy. And the social teaching of their officials over the years on specific issues has clearly demonstrated the same.

Learning from the Past

Catholic colonists, as before noted, came to Maryland and received specific religious toleration there. However, the original policy of toleration toward Catholics was not consistently followed in that colony. Restrictions on the political liberty of Catholics were also imposed in other colonies. In Pennsylvania there was consistent religious toleration, and the first growth of the Catholic Church was made in that colony and in Maryland.

Father John Carroll, who became the first bishop in the United States, could write in 1787, four years after the close of the Revolutionary War, and two years before the Constitution went into effect: "Thanks to genuine spirit and Christianity, the United States have banished intolerance from their system of government, and many of them have done the justice to every denomination of Christians, which ought to be done to them in all, of placing them on the same footing of citizenship, and conferring an equal right of participation in national privileges. Freedom and independence, acquired by united efforts, and cemented with the mingled blood of Protestant and Catholic fellow-citizens, should be equally enjoyed by all." [1]

The Plenary Council of Bishops held at Baltimore, 1884, issued a pastoral letter that included the following: "We think we can claim to be acquainted with the laws, institutions, and spirit of the Catholic Church, and with the laws, institutions, and spirit of our country; and we emphatically declare that there is no antagonism between them. . . . We believe that our country's heroes were the instruments of the God of Nations in establishing this home of freedom; to both the Almighty and to His instruments in the work we look with grateful reverence; and to maintain the inheritance of freedom which they have left us, should it ever—which God forbid—be imperiled, our Catholic citizens will be able to stand forward, as one man, ready to pledge anew 'their lives, their fortunes, and their sacred honor.' " [2]

In 1919 the bishops of the United States in a pastoral letter declared: "With great wisdom our American constitution provides that every citizen shall be free to follow the dictates of his conscience in the matter of religious belief and observance. While the state gives no preference to any form of religion, its own best interests require that religion as well as education should flourish and exert its wholesome influence upon the lives of the people. And since education is so powerful an agency for the preservation of religion, equal freedom should be secured to both."

The 1960 Presidential Campaign

The 1960 Presidential campaign, in which Senator John F. Kennedy of Massachusetts was the successful candidate, aroused broad discussion of religious liberty. As in 1928 fears were expressed that a President with membership in the Roman Catholic Church could not be committed fully to religious liberty for all, and that he could not exercise the necessary independence of his Church. Much anti-Catholic literature was circulated, reminiscent of the campaign of 1928, when Governor Alfred E. Smith of New York was the unsuccessful candidate. However, the then Senator Kennedy conducted his campaign in a spirit far different from that of Governor Smith. He freely discussed religious liberty and the closely related matter of separation of church and state. (See Chapter 10, "John F. Kennedy, Catholic.")

There were also joint expressions by Protestants, Orthodox, Jews, and Roman Catholics that showed a high degree of consensus among many officials of these bodies with respect to religious liberty. One of these statements, notable for its clarity and forthright expression, was signed by more than a hundred churchmen and scholars in the "four faiths." Although they all signed only in their personal capacities, they were undoubtedly also spokesmen for large sections of their own constituencies. Among the twenty-nine Roman Catholics signing were Richard Cardinal Cushing of Boston; Archbishop Robert E. Lucey of San Antonio; Bishop Robert J. Dwyer of Reno; Monsignor Edward G. Murray of Roslindale, Massachusetts; Robert F. Drinan, S.J., of Boston College Law School; Monsignor Timothy J. Flynn, of New York; Reverend John Courtney Murray, S.J., of Woodstock College, Maryland; Reverend Thurston J. Davis, editor of *America;* Reverend John LaFarge, S.J., an associate editor of *America.* Among well-known Catholic laymen signing were George N. Shuster, former president of Hunter College; Harry J. Carman, former dean of Columbia College; Carlton J. H. Hayes, former ambassador of the United States to Spain.

The text of the statement entitled "Religious Liberty and the 1960 Campaign," made public, September 12, 1960, and published in many newspapers and periodicals, read in part:

"Every person must be accorded full religious liberty, and no person shall be coerced into accepting any religious faith or practice. No religious group should be given special preference or advantage by the state, nor allowed to use state agencies for the restriction of other faiths."

Recent Discussions

More recent discussions were greatly influenced by statements in the encyclical, *Pacem in Terris* (*Peace on Earth*), issued in 1963 by Pope John XXIII. The Pope gave specific approval to the Universal Declaration of Human Rights adopted unanimously by the General Assembly of the United Nations in 1948, which contains the following: "Everyone has the right to freedom of thought, conscience, and religion; this right includes freedom to change his religion or belief, and freedom, either alone or in community with others and in public or private, to manifest his religion or belief in teaching, practice, worship, and observance." The Pope's own words in the encyclical were: "Every human being has the right to honor God according to the dictates of an upright conscience, and therefore the right to worship God privately and publicly."

In 1963 a proposed statement on religious liberty never reached the Second Vatican Council for debate. In 1964, the issues involved were again among the warmest. In the closing week of the session the Council Presidents (cardinals) first recommended that the Council itself should decide whether it wished to vote or not. Then, apparently after pressure from the conservative wing, the Council Presidents decided that there would be no vote at all. This aroused Cardinals Ritter and Meyer of the United States and Léger from Canada, who secured over 1,000 signatures on a petition to the Pope asking him to intervene and order a vote. The Pope did not intervene. The result was a great disappointment to Protestants and others who had great expectations from the Council; also "depression" and "resentment" within the Council.

Thus the Council declined to repeat what John XXIII had said in *Pacem in Terris* (*Peace on Earth*), 1963. However, the fact that a majority of the members present had signed a hurriedly arranged petition, and that there was an international furore over religious liberty, were both good evidence of broad interest. It seems the main opposition came from the nations (e.g., Italy and Spain) where the Catholic Church has a position of preference from the state. In 1965, by a vote of nine to one, the Council gave preliminary approval to a declaration favoring choice of religion for all in accord with conscience.

10

John F. Kennedy, Catholic

John Fitzgerald Kennedy (1917–1963) was the first President of the United States who was a Catholic. He was not "the first Catholic President," as his words and behavior made abundantly clear, despite the popular use of this phrase. His political career was most distinguished and unique. He attained the Presidency in spite of the past positions of the people that they would not have a President who was a Catholic, even though the Constitution has always plainly said that there shall be no religious test for public office in the nation. His campaign for the Vice Presidency in 1956 and that for the Presidency in 1960 demonstrated that he was a master in the school of politics. Great were his distinction and brilliance as a public figure and servant, and so were his talents in the service of his Church. He contributed to his Church both directly and indirectly, but always openly and frankly. He was plainly, without saying it, an educator of the American public with respect to the nature and genius of the religious institution to which he belonged.

A Biographical Note

John Fitzgerald Kennedy, 35th President of the United States, was born in Brookline, Massachusetts, May 29, 1917. He was the son of Joseph Patrick and Rose (Fitzgerald) Kennedy. He received the degree of B.S., *cum laude,* from Harvard University in 1940. He served in the United States Navy, 1941–1945, and was decorated by the Navy and the Marine Corps with the Purple Heart Medal. He married Jacqueline Lee Bouvier, September 12, 1953. They had three children, Caroline Bouvier, John Fitzgerald, and Patrick Bouvier (deceased). He became a candidate of the Democratic Party and was elected in 1947 as the Representative of the 11th Massachusetts District in Congress, serving until 1953. He was U.S. Senator from Massachusetts, 1953–61. He was elected a member of the Board of Overseers of Harvard University in 1957. He was the author of the following books: *Why England Slept,* 1940; *Profiles in Courage,* 1956 (awarded the Pulitzer Prize for biography in 1957); *Strategy of Peace,* 1960. He was elected President of the United States in November, 1960, serving until he was assassinated on November 22, 1963, at Dallas, Texas. His body was interred at Arlington Cemetery.

"The Tribune of the People"

Until 1960, Roman Catholics had served well as justices of the Supreme Court of the United States, as elected members of the House of Representatives and as Senators. As judges they were found competent to interpret the laws of the land; as members of Congress they were regarded as able to initiate and to vote on pending measures. The people had regarded the Presidency as something decidedly "different"—in spite of the words in the Constitution. Probably many people felt the Presidency was different because of one of the facets of the office, which has been called the "grandest institution in the world," is that of "tribune of the people." One of the numerous duties of the President (who must be many men) is that he is the representative of the American people to the world. The office is a symbol of the people. Thus, it seems to have been generally held, he should be from the largest religious group. This overwhelming sentiment ran counter, of course, to another popular idea that "every boy" should obviously have the opportunity to become President. Thus we were plainly contradictory—our Presidents must be white, Anglo-Saxon Protestants, or of that tradition, while the office was theoretically open to the humblest in origin.

The Presidential Campaign of 1928

Hanging over Senator Kennedy's aspirations were memories of the Presidential campaign of 1928, when Alfred E. Smith, Governor of New York, and a prominent Roman Catholic, was the Democratic candidate. The concern of many, perhaps most, Protestants was then surely aroused. A number of assemblies of Protestant bodies went formally on record in opposition to Governor Smith, who was obviously in the conservative wing of his party, just as Herbert Hoover was among the Republicans.

The Protestant religious press seems almost unanimously to have opposed Governor Smith. *The Christian Century*, Chicago, an undenominational journal with subscribers among the ministers and lay people from a number of Protestant denominations, said editorially, October 11, 1928: "The anti-Catholic voter is opposed to the occupancy of the White House by a Roman Catholic because he sees, or thinks he sees, a real issue between Catholicism and American institutions. It involves the exercise of just as much intelligence to discern and to define this issue as the same voter would put into his consideration of the equalization fee, or water power, or the tariff, or prohibition, or any other issue." In declining to vote for a candidate who is a Catholic, the voter "is not acting as an intolerant person, or a bigot, but as an intelligent and faithful American citizen."

There were, of course, other Protestant arguments. One very conservative Protestant clergyman said that he and many others would have regarded the then Senator Thomas J. Walsh, of Montana, a Roman Catholic and a "dry" as a most acceptable candidate. Rural versus urban conflicts also figured in the campaign. Mr. Smith was from the sidewalks of New York, of recent immigrant stock, a member of Tammany Hall, a "wet," and a Roman Catholic.

The Ku Klux Klan was rampant in 1928. Its huge parades of hooded men had great political influence, and the Klan was anti-Catholic as well as anti-Jew and anti-Negro.

Approaching the 1960 Campaign

After a surprisingly good showing as a candidate for the nomination for the office of Vice President in the Democratic Convention in 1956, Senator Kennedy began conducting a quiet and well-organized campaign for the Presidential nomination in 1960. And his religious affiliation was at once publicly discussed. For example, the National Broadcasting Company conducted a panel discussion on "Religion and the Presidency" as early as June 1, 1958.

Two of the participants, evidently opposed to election of a candidate who was a Catholic, spoke much as *The Christian Century* had declared itself in 1928: "American institutions" might be endangered or weakened by a Roman Catholic. Church and state might not remain separate. A Roman Catholic in the White House might not be as free a man as a Jew or a Protestant. A President with a Catholic affiliation might appoint an ambassador to the Vatican. Such a President might espouse private religious schools to an extent that the public school systems would be weakened.

A Protestant clergyman on the panel said, on the other hand, that "Roman Catholics have served as faithfully and as openly as any other public servants." Roman Catholics owe an allegiance, not to a foreign power, but to God; and this allegiance to God is essentially no different from that of Protestants generally.

A member of the House of Representatives, a Roman Catholic who had been a college teacher, said that since the Constitution forbids a religious test for public office, the same standards should apply to all candidates. Both the state and the church have their proper spheres, functions, and objectives. The two cannot be "absolutely" separated (echoing an opinion also held by many non-Catholics). The church must express some concern for the temporal welfare of man, and the state has "some responsibility and concern for religion."

Senator Kennedy Discusses Religion

Senator Kennedy, before he had publicly declared his candidacy, met the whole issue in a frontal statement in an interview in *Look* magazine, March 3, 1959, where he was quoted as follows:

"I am flatly opposed to appointment of an ambassador to the Vatican. Whatever advantages it might have in Rome—and I'm not convinced of these—they would be more than offset by the divisive effect at home.

"The First Amendment to the Constitution is an infinitely wise one. There can be no question of Federal funds being used for support of parochial or private schools. It's unconstitutional under the First Amendment as interpreted by the Supreme Court. I'm opposed to the Federal Government's extending support to sustain any church or its schools. As for such fringe matters as buses, lunches and other services, the issue is primarily social and economic and not religious. Each case must be judged on its merits within the law as interpreted by the courts."

Senator Kennedy also said: "Whatever one's religion in his private life may be, for the officeholder, nothing takes precedence over his oath to uphold the Constitution and all its parts—including the First Amendment and the strict separation of Church and State."

The 1960 Campaign

Senator Kennedy conducted his 1960 Presidential campaign with a clear recognition of the religious issue. He consented to speak before a forum convened by the Protestant Ministerial Association of Houston, Texas. There he answered all questions fully and respectfully, with maturity and perspective. Most of the questions were of the same nature as those answered in the *Look* interview. Mr. Kennedy's references to religion, which were not frequent in the campaign, were in a spirit of inquiry and frankness probably not attained by the candidate who was a Catholic in 1928. Mr. Kennedy must have been elected, in a very close vote, with the enthusiastic support of many non-Catholics, some of whom must have been eager to put an end to the tradition that the United States must not have a President affiliated with the Roman Catholic Church.

The Christian Century of 1960 spoke in a tone quite different from that of 1928. None of the 1928 arguments was advanced. The editors spoke respectfully of Senator Kennedy, indicating that he could become a good President. The Protestant religious press, never unanimous on any great issue, included many publications other than *The Christian Century* that could see no danger to American institutions in the candidacy of Senator Kennedy. The anti-Catholic political pamphleteering of 1960 was again very widespread. Some 390 pieces of such literature have been gathered up by one researcher alone. Dr. Patricia Barrett, a professor of political science at the Maryville campus of St. Louis University, has documented and analyzed this mass of hate, fear, and suspicion, with the advice of both Protestant and Catholic advisers, in the book, *Religious Liberty and the American Presidency*.[1] It appears evident from this study that large sections of the American people either circulated or believed the theses of the pamphleteering, which were undoubtedly repudiated by a high proportion of Protestant officials of the nation. Dr. Barrett recommended more authentic and extensive "dialogue" between Catholics and others.

Mr. Kennedy and His Church

To the Houston Protestant ministers, Senator Kennedy reiterated his conviction that he saw no conflict between his Catholic conscience and the oath of public office. He knew that he must be aware of his Catholicism during the campaign and later as President.

He knew that he was no theologian and said so a number of times. Yet he had a fine grasp of Catholic teaching and morality, and it can be said that he "served his Church as brilliantly as he served his country," as John Cogley, then a staff member of the Center for the Study of Democratic Institutions, put it in *The Commonweal*.[2]

After he became President the "school issue" in relation to "the religious issue" at once came up. He knew that many Catholics favored Federal funds for support of private, including parochial, elementary, and secondary schools. He consistently said that, as he read recent Supreme Court opinions, such grants would be unconstitutional. Yet despite this position, and his lack of interest in abstract theological thought, "John F. Kennedy probably had more influence on the future of the American Church than any Catholic, lay or clerical, in the history of the nation," in the words of Mr. Cogley, a well-informed Catholic layman.

Three reasons were cited in support of this generalization:

First, "the sheer facts of his life." "He was the quintessential modern man, a product of the twentieth century, gifted with a good mind, a graduate of the most respected schools, a sophisticate, and a universally admired statesman." He wore both his Catholicism and his modernity elegantly. He was a man of unspectacular loyalty to his Church. He was when he died a hero to many Americans, especially young Americans.

Second, he taught through his career that the American Catholic Church had recognized and come to grips with "religious pluralism" (or diversity) in our society.

Third, he helped to rescue politics from the disdain with which it has often been held among the American people. He demonstrated responsible use of power in a complex society.

11

Public Policy Positions
of American Catholics

"The Negro problem is upon us, and there is no other solution to it, peaceful and permanent, than to grant to our colored citizens practical and effective equality with white citizens . . . I would break down all barriers. Let the Negro be our equal before the law . . . I claim the rights I grant to others, and my door is opened to men of all colors . . . Social equality is a matter of taste; the granting of it largely depends on our elevation above prejudice, and the identification of minds and hearts with the precepts and the counsels of the Gospel." [1]

The lines above are from a sermon by Archbishop John Ireland of St. Paul, January 1, 1891. In August, 1964, Richard Cardinal Cushing spoke in a similar tenor, referring to riots of Negroes in cities. It is the responsibility of white persons to move effectively toward elimination of "the monstrous evils of racism from our lives, our cities, and our nation." "All men of goodwill should be in favor of freedom, full freedom for his [the Negro's] every right as a man and as a citizen." "We have required a superhuman patience of the American Negro and when this has proved too much for his tortured person, we have been dismayed because he has answered with an excess of agitation the longer excesses of neglect. How else can he answer except in outrage the society that marks him as inferior to his fellowman?" [2]

The Roman Catholic Bishops of the United States, in August, 1963, issued a joint pastoral letter declaring against all forms of discrimination and segregation "by sole fact of race and regardless of individual qualities." They were simply reiterating, they noted, what they had said in 1940 and 1958.

Racial Equality

Thus official Catholic policy is favorable to equal rights and dignity for all races. This is also the official public position of most religious bodies in the United States. Implementation of bold social ideals encounters the same practical difficulties in the Catholic Church as elsewhere in organized religion. Many members do not read the declarations of their officials. Not all bishops implement with the same zeal the specific moral judgments declared by all bishops in conference. Indeed, there is good evidence that one cardinal does not do much to implement ideas of racial equality. So it is in the parishes. Much depends upon the behavior and attitude of the priest in charge. Apparently not all priests read carefully the words on racial equality appearing in the encyclical, *Peace on Earth*, by Pope John XXIII. Years ago a Pope is reported to have observed that the "man in the street" was not at all aware of the communications of the Pope.

A number of the positions on public policy have already been noted in the preceding chapters. Here, only brief summaries of those matters will be given, while those not mentioned before will be treated at greater length.

Economic Issues

Beginning with Pope Leo XIII in his encyclical *Rerum Novarum* (*On the Condition of Labor*), 1891, and the

American Catholic *Bishops' Program of Social Reconstruction,* 1919, the Catholic Church may accurately be described as "pioneering" in declaring right relationships in the economy. Leo XIII, of an aristocratic family, nevertheless moved official Catholic thought out of the confines of Italian and European aristocracies. He understood the significance of the rise of the urban industrial workers, and also the importance of their organization. Thus the right of labor—as well as employers—to organize was approved by the Pope in 1891. He also touched on many other matters, such as a just wage, the right of private property, and the desirability of its wide diffusion among the people. This declaration came at a time when most religious bodies of the United States were officially indifferent or somnolent with respect to the labor movement. Only a few alert Protestant theologians in the United States sensed that Leo was writing in a strain far different from that of any other churchman.

Immediately after World War I, "social reconstruction" was often discussed by officials of religious bodies. One of the official pronouncements, which probably received more public attention than any other, was the *Bishops' Program of Social Reconstruction,* adopted, 1919, by the National Catholic War Council (later renamed the National Catholic Welfare Conference). The bishops said they hoped to state "the lines that will best guide us." The "essential declarations are based upon the principles of charity and justice that have always been held and taught by the Catholic Church . . ."

Among the points advocated by the bishops were these:

"The several states should enact laws providing for the establishment of wage rates at least sufficient for the decent maintenance of a family in the case of all male adults, and adequate to the decent individual support of female workers. . . . We are glad to note that there is no longer any serious objection urged by impartial persons against the legal minimum wage."

"The State should make comprehensive provision for insurance against illness, invalidity, unemployment, and old age." (This proposal was *not* in the program recommended by the Committee on Reconstruction of the American Federation of Labor, issued at about the same time.)

"More important and more effective than any government regulation of prices would be the establishment of cooperative stores . . . This is no Utopian scheme. It has been successfully carried out in England and Scotland through the Rochdale system. The cooperative stores would train our working people and consumers generally in habits of saving, in careful expenditure, in business methods . . .

"The right of labor to organize and to deal with employers through representatives" had been so frequently recognized during World War I that "this right will never again be called in question by any considerable number of employers."

Adopting a recommendation of a group of English Quaker employers, the bishops said that labor had not only the right to organize but also to ask for participation in "business management," such as determination of hours of work, of work rules, of "nature of the product," welfare work, etc.

Child labor should be abolished by "taxing" it "out of existence." The precise method approved was a Federal revenue bill that "would impose a tax of 10 per cent on all goods made by children."

Vocational training "should be made substantially universal."

For "excessive gains by a small minority of privileged capitalists, the main remedies are prevention of monopolistic control of commodities, adequate government regulation of such public service monopolies as will remain under private operation, and heavy taxation of incomes, excess profits, and inheritances."

" 'Society can be healed in no other way than by a return to Christian life and Christian institutions,' " said the bishops, quoting Leo XIII. Both labor and employers needed to acquire new attitudes and spirit.

The conclusion was: "Labor's right to a decent livelihood is the first moral charge upon industry. The employer has a right to get a reasonable living out of his business, but he has no right to interest on his investment until his employees have obtained at least living wages. This is the human and Christian, in contrast to the purely commercial and pagan, ethics of industry."

Reconstructing the Social Order

Pius XI issued in 1931, forty years after Leo's *Rerum Novarum* (*On the Condition of Labor*), an encyclical with the Latin name, *Quadragesimo Anno* known as *Reconstructing the Social Order*. He wrote in one of the opening paragraphs: "Before proceeding to discuss these problems, we lay down the principles long since already established by Leo XIII, that it is Our right and duty to deal authoritatively with social and economic problems. It is not, of course, the office of the Church to lead men to transient and perishable happiness only but to that which is eternal . . . But she never can relinquish her God-given task of interposing her authority, not indeed in technical matters, for which she has neither the equipment nor the mission, but in all those that have a bearing on moral conduct. For the deposit of truth entrusted to us by God, and our weighty office of propagating, interpreting, and urging in season and out of season the entire moral law, demand that both social and economic questions be brought within Our supreme jurisdiction, in so far as they refer to moral issues . . ."

Pius XI then emphasized, among others, the recommendation that "workers and officials become participants in ownership or management, or share in some manner in profits." He stated that the views of Communists and Christians are radically opposed. He suggested the following general principles: In determining wages, justice requires that, in addition to the needs of the individual worker and his family, regard be had on the one hand for conditions within the productive enterprises wherein workers labor; on the other hand, for the "public economic good . . ." The self-organization of all economic groups is to be encouraged. There is need for international economic cooperation.

Christianity and Social Progress

In 1961, seventy years after Leo XIII wrote on social and economic matters, John XXIII published his encyclical, *Mater et Magistra* (*Christianity and Social Progress*). It is comprehensive and sums up many of the social principles expressed by Popes in the past; it also goes in some detail into matters not often previously stated. The newer positions are those in favor of assistance for the underdeveloped nations, the proper role of "public property," and "socialization."

There are now "world dimensions of every important human problem," the Pope wrote. The wealthier nations should provide "scientific, technical, and financial cooperation" to the less developed nations. This should be done without "colonialism" and with due respect for the special characteristics of the nations being aided. The Pontiff specifically approved the "highly beneficial" work of the Food and Agriculture Organization of the United Nations.

Farming, a subject seldom dealt with directly by previous Popes, was called a "depressed sector" of the economies of the world. Rural people should be provided with public and social services equal to those of urban areas, and they should also have access to social insurance systems. Enterprises operated by families should have conditions that permit "living in decent comfort." It is also indispensable that farmers organize a "flourishing system of cooperative undertakings." The Pope expressed "satisfaction with Our sons in various parts of the world who are actively engaged in cooperatives, in professional groups, and worker movements, with a view to raising the economic and social standards of rural workers."

The right to own private property is fully stated, also the view that it should be broadly held, and that it has duties to society. The state also has the right lawfully to possess productive goods, but public property is "subsidiary" to private property.

In our times one of the typical aspects of societies is "socialization." This is "understood as the progressive multiplication of relations in society." "Socialization is, at one and the same time, an effect and a cause of growing intervention of the public authorities in even the most crucial matters." It is also an expression of desires of peoples "to join together to attain objectives which are beyond the capacity and means at the disposal of single individuals." The results may bring many advantages and satisfy many human rights, if the process is limited and controlled in a responsible way for economic and social development.

"Heartfelt appreciation to the International Labor Organization" of the United Nations was expressed. Industrial workers generally should be paid a wage "which allows them to live a truly human life and face up with dignity to their family responsibilities." They have the right not only to form their own organizations but also to participate "in the ownership of the enterprise itself." Artisans and craftsmen should also organize "cooperative enterprises."

Peace on Earth

Perhaps the most widely noted encyclical of modern times was that of *Pacem in Terris* (*Peace on Earth*), April, 1963, issued by Pope John after the first session of the Second Vatican Council and only a few months before his death. It was studied and favorably received by statesmen and religious leaders throughout the world. The Unitarian Universalist Association, for example, formally declared it a most important statement.

The Pope specifically approved the purposes and methods of the United Nations, and also praised its Universal Declaration of Human Rights. When he did this, at least one Catholic lay organization in the United States was openly campaigning against the United Nations. His favorable words on the Declaration of Human Rights were also significant because one of its sections reads: "Everyone has the right to freedom of thought, conscience and religion; this right includes freedom to change his religion or belief, and freedom, either alone or in community with others and in public or private, to manifest his religion or belief in teaching, practice, worship and observance."

Pope John's bold and courageous encyclicals and other public statements on international cooperation did not win for him unanimous applause either within the Curia or among the diverse laity of the Church throughout the world. In the United States, however, hearty applause seemed to drown out dissent, both within and without the Catholic Church. The Catholic Bishops of the United States have surely been consistent supporters of the United Nations. "The United Nations," the bishops declared in

1956, "offers the only present promise we have for sustained peace in our time; peace with any approximation of justice."

Other Positions

In other chapters of this book, it is stated that Catholics in the United States, generally and officially,

Favor:

Federal aid to private (including parochial) elementary and secondary schools.

Family limitation only by delayed marriage, continence, or periodic continence by use of the rhythm method.

Religious liberty for all religious bodies.

Separation of church and state, with no privileged position for any religious body.

Complete church charities or social services for neglected and handicapped children.

Use of English in many portions of the Mass and administration of sacraments; other methods to encourage the laity to take part in the liturgy.

Reading by the laity of Bible versions approved by the Church.

New translations of the Scriptures under episcopal supervision.

Strict and limited public laws with respect to divorce.

Intermarriage only under specific regulation of the Church.

Adoption of children by religious affiliation of parents.

Many officials and students of all faiths seem to agree that the Roman Catholic Church often declares itself specifically on social, economic, and international policies and reforms; and that this is done more unitedly, and probably more impressively, than by most other large religious bodies in the United States.

12

The Papacy
in Modern Perspective

When Angelo Cardinal Roncalli of Venice was elected Pope in the fall of 1958, he chose the name of John XXIII, and explained why he had done so. John was the name of his father; it was the name of the parish in the village where he was baptized; it was the name chosen by more Popes than any other; thus he could hide his own smallness within the grandeur of those with this name that had gone before him. He was, of course, as mistaken as Abraham Lincoln at Gettysburg who said that the world would little note nor long remember what he said there. For from the moment when Angelo Roncalli was elected Pope, the name of John grew in greatness.

The Emergence of Good Pope John

John XXIII made the Papacy known throughout the world, as it had probably not been recognized for a long time, because of his personality, his words, and his actions. His wit and wisdom, the legends told by press, by associates, and by grapevine, his generous attitude toward those of other faiths, all these also contributed to the world's appreciation.

It was not unusual during a public audience held by the Pope for a peasant woman to say spontaneously: "He *is* one of us." He did speak well to peasants, but he was also able to communicate with all sorts and conditions of

119

persons. He was a sturdy descendant of farmers of the north of Italy, and his relatives appeared in Rome for his coronation laden with good sausages for him from the north, which they said were far superior to the food available in Rome.

There were cardinals voting in 1958, it seems well established, who expected a quiet regime during which relatively little would be attempted. Instead, they had elected a man with unusual insight and courage. This was revealed by incidents as well as by the actions with worldwide significance. Once when the Pope strolled through the Vatican gardens, a workman altogether naturally approached to do homage. A guard stepped between the Pope and the workman. The Pope inquired of the guard why he had acted. For security reasons, was the explanation. The Pope then asked: "Did you think that I would harm him?"

One day in January, 1960, the Pope decided to take a walk in the streets of Rome. When asked why, he said he had been reading that up to about a hundred years ago the Popes had strolled in the city—there was a hoary precedent. He shocked the police of the city, "for security reasons," but the people of Rome applauded. At a pushcart, the Pope asked the vendor for a cookie, sampled it, then recalled that the Pope carries no money. The owner solved the problem by asking the Pope to accept his complete stock of cookies, and to take them with him into the Vatican.

To a group of Jews entering his study for an audience, the Pope said: "I am your brother."

When a churchman not of the Roman Catholic faith came from an audience, he was asked what might be the result of the visit. The reply was that when there is so much love in the heart of a man as there was in John XXIII, no one can tell what the result will be.

"We are not friars singing in a choir," explained the Supreme Head of his Church when he was asked about the warm debates among the some 2,500 bishops attending the first session of the Second Vatican Council in 1962. To an associate who intimated that perhaps the Pope did not know how to run a Council, he is reported to have given one of his more refreshing replies. He knew that he did not know how to run a Council, but then neither did his interrogator nor anyone else. Nobody in Rome in 1962 had participated in the First Vatican Council of 1869–1870.

To officials of religious bodies of many faiths and to the statesmen of the world, John XXIII became known especially for two of his encyclicals, *Mater et Magistra* (*Christianity and Social Progress*), 1961, published seventy years after Leo XIII issued *Rerum Novarum* (*On the Condition of Labor*), and *Pacem in Terris* (*Peace on Earth*), 1963; and for the calling of the Second Vatican Council. (For an account of the Council, see Chapter 14, "Second Vatican Council."

Christianity and Social Progress opened with a summary of what the predecessor Popes had said on the social order. John XXIII reemphasized the importance of private ownership of property and of its wide diffusion among the people; and of self-organization of economic groups and vocations. Yet there is a proper socialization, or public intervention in economic and social life. This can bring many advantages. In modern society there is also much public property; this can be beneficial when the public authority, the state, is subject to wise and constant inspection by the citizens. Agriculture is called a depressed sector of the world economy, requiring special methods of improvement through government and voluntary cooperation. The Pope restated the traditional opposition to birth control by artificial means (contraceptives or drugs) as a means of dealing with the pressure of rapidly increasing populations on food and other resources.

In *Peace on Earth* he shocked some Roman Catholics and pleased many others of his Church and elsewhere by his unequivocal approval of the aims and procedures of the United Nations. He said that in the modern world some forms of international public authority are needed. He also approved the Universal Declaration of Human Rights adopted unanimously by the General Assembly of the United Nations in 1948 as a standard for all people.

A few months after his election, while the Pope was at prayer, the thought came to him that he should convene a Council of all the bishops of the Church throughout the world. He seems to have announced that there would be an Ecumenical Council without consulting widely among the efficient and experienced advisers and associates in the Curia. There is good evidence that most of them were not pleased with a plan for broad discussions of important issues. The Pope said that the affairs of the Roman Catholic Church would have the primary emphasis, but that indirectly there might be influences that would eventually make for unity with "the separated brethren."

To an associate who reported that because of the mass of details involved in preparation the Council could not possibly be convened as early as 1963, the Pope said then it would be held in 1962. The Council opened in October, 1962.

When the Pope lay dying in the spring of 1963, the London correspondent of *The New Yorker* recorded the awareness of the people of England of the Pope's suffering and of the words he had spoken to them. This was a people traditionally suspicious, even apathetic, toward the Papacy. But he had addressed to them words that they wanted to hear, and they were expressing their grief.

In the United States the feelings were much the same.

Lutherans and Presbyterians, for example, acclaimed the Pope as one of the influential men of his time. When word of the Pope's death came, a Protestant official said he wished he could head a committee to start a movement to have John XXIII declared a saint. As this is written, thousands of Roman Catholics have already taken the initial steps. This was the man who was expected to head a "caretaker" regime.

In the paragraphs above the career of one man has been interpreted to illustrate important aspects of the Papacy today. Now follows an outline of the origin of the Church in Rome and of a number of events in the course of epochs in the long history of the Papacy.

Rome—A Center of the Early Church

The Papacy is a term applied to the office of the Bishop of Rome, the Pope, with reference to both his ecclesiastical authority as Supreme Ruler of the Church, as ruler of the former Papal States, and now as governor of Vatican City. The origins of this office, or institution, are traced to the small group of Christians who gathered in Rome in the early years of the Apostolic Church, probably in the period, A.D. 41–54. Rome was a center of broad commerce and communication, and undoubtedly Christians from many parts of the Mediterranean made their way to the city for many reasons. Evidence of its importance to the Apostles was Paul's letter to the Romans, in which he summed up many of the essentials of the Christian faith.

The Book of Acts records that Paul was a prisoner in Rome. In the writings of the Church Fathers evidence is given that Peter also went there. Both Peter and Paul are believed to have been martyrs there. Other early Apostolic Churches in the Mediterranean area were also important.

But the Church in Jerusalem and that in other cities seem not to have exerted strong leadership. Because Peter and Paul had died in Rome, their tombs were honored there. Rome became truly the center of the Graeco-Roman world. For about four centuries it was also the center of the Christian Church, despite schisms and disputes. Then there arose strong church centers at Constantinople, Antioch, Alexandria, and Carthage; and the center in Rome came to be somewhat separated from Christianity in the Greek world. Also, in Italy, Milan became a place of political, economic, and ecclesiastical importance. Finally, Constantinople became the center of ecclesiastical authority of the Byzantine area.

However, pilgrimage to Rome continued through the centuries to be one of the most important of Christian venerations. Pilgrims came to pay their respects to the tombs of St. Peter and St. Paul. And the Bishop of Rome was the guardian of those tombs.

An Outline of Epochs of the Papacy

Events in the Papacy are sometimes summed up in most general terms in a number of epochs as follows:

I. From Apostolic Days to Gregory VII (*ca.* A.D. 50–1085). This included the term of Gregory I or the Great (A.D. 590–604). He sent missions to England. The churches of Gaul, Germany, and England attained vitality. Learning was encouraged. In this epoch occurred the final break between the Greek East and the Roman West, generally dated at 1054, over the wording of the Nicene Creed and the authority of the Pope. The temporal power of the Pope, which began with private gifts of land about A.D. 750 was greatly extended, and the Pope became the temporal ruler of a large section of Italy named the Papal States. This epoch ended with the rule of Gregory VII (1073–

1085), who was a reformer. He sought the free election of a Pope by the Church, without the intervention of secular rulers.

II. 1085–1124. Gregory's successors continued efforts to free the Church from feudal domination. One of the outstanding figures was Urban II (1088–1099), a Frenchman who was probably more vigorous than Gregory VII. The foundation of the Papacy as both religious and temporal power became well established. This was also the era of the first two of the Christian Crusades against the Saracens of the East, for the purpose of freeing the Holy Places of Palestine. Urged on by Urban II the city of Jerusalem was taken by Western Crusaders after armed action between 1096 and 1099. Later, when the Mesopotamian city of Edessa fell into Moslem hands, Western emperors took the cross again in 1147, but this venture ended in failure a year later.

III. 1124–1198. In the twelfth century the Popes consolidated their authority. Two Popes had relatively long reigns: Innocent II (1130–1143), and Alexander III (1159–1181). A really centralized organization was set up in Rome. The Third Crusade, 1187–1198, was begun against the Moslems, but when it ended Jerusalem was still in Saracen hands.

IV. 1198–1261. As the authority of the Popes was centralized, disputes and conflicts with the civil powers resulted. Universities were encouraged. This is known as one of the grand epochs. Prominent Popes were Innocent III (1198–1216); Honorius III (1216–1218); Gregory IX (1227–1241). Innocent III launched the Fourth Crusade in 1202–1204, which ended inconclusively. The Fifth Crusade went on for many years from 1217 on, during which Jerusalem changed hands several times, and the period ended in a truce.

V. 1261–1305. There were thirteen Popes, all with relatively short reigns. The influence of France on the Papacy became great. There were minor Crusades against the Moslems, but none to the extent of the first five.

VI. 1305–1590. Pope Gascon Clement V (1305–1314), former Archbishop of Bordeaux, remained in France. There were schisms, and at one time three persons professed to be Pope. There were "political popes." The Protestant Reformation began under the leadership of a German monk, Martin Luther, in 1517, during the term of Leo X (1513–1521). The Council of Trent was held at intervals between 1545 and 1563, where the Counter Reformation was organized. The Congregation of the Inquisition was set up in Rome in 1542. Strenuous efforts for "Catholic Restoration" were carried out from 1566 to 1590.

VII. 1590–1900. The work of restoration went on. The Age of Enlightenment created great intellectual and theological problems, because of revolts of intellectuals against ecclesiastical authority. The French Revolution in the 1790's was in part a move against the Church. The revolutions of 1848 shook the entire continent of Europe. Italian nationalism called for a united Italy, and the Papal States fell before Italian arms in 1870. The Pope then went as a sort of "prisoner" into the Vatican. (The Popes remained there until 1929, when a treaty with Italy was negotiated.)

Papal infallibility was declared and defined by the First Vatican Council, 1869–1870. The pertinent wording reads: "Faithfully adhering to the tradition received from the beginning of the Christian faith . . . we teach and define that it is a dogma divinely revealed that the Roman pontiff, when he speaks *ex cathedra,* that is, when in discharge of the office of pastor and teacher of all Christians, by virtue of his supreme Apostolic authority, he defines a doctrine, regarding faith and morals to be held by the universal church, by the divine assistance promised him in the Blessed Peter, is possessed of that infallibility with which the Divine Redeemer willed that His Church should be endowed for defining doctrine regarding faith and morals; and that, therefore, such definitions of the Roman Pontiffs are irreformable of themselves and not from the consent of the Church." [1]

The debate on the issue was long and intense. The first vote is reported to have been 451 in favor, 88 opposed, 62 conditionally in favor. The final vote was 433 in favor, 2 opposing, 55 abstaining. Several bishops at once withdrew from the Roman Catholic Church and formed the Old Catholic bodies in the Netherlands, Germany, and Switzerland. The non-Catholic religious world generally took a serious view, holding that the new dogma would hinder contacts and cooperation between the Roman Catholic Church and other bodies. The governments of France, Great Britain, Spain, and Portugal issued formal memoranda expressing regret. Germany and Austria also expressed disapproval.

Leo XIII, in office from 1878 to 1903, became in the opinion of many the first modern Pope. He encouraged the reading of the Bible, became a patron of the arts, favored the founding of the Catholic University in Washington, D.C., expressed himself as in accord with the aspirations of industrial workers for effective organization and for a just and living wage, declared Thomism (teachings of St. Thomas Aquinas) to be the official philosophy of his Church. He was surely one of the most versatile of the Popes.

VIII. The twentieth century. Saint Pius X succeeded Leo XIII, and served from 1903 to 1914. He was always predominantly a pastor, and even when Pope found time to hear confessions. During his term he made a broad condemnation of "modernism" in thought and philosophy, mentioning sixty-five principles held by intellectuals and liberal non-Catholic theologians. For this he received much attention throughout the world, and considerable opposition from intellectuals and Protestants. Toward the end of his life he strove in vain to avoid the great conflict of World War I. He died but a few weeks before the fighting began.

Benedict XV, who had been Archbishop of Bologna, was made a cardinal only a few months before he was elected Pope in 1914. He served until his death in 1922. During World War I he tried to observe the strictest neutrality. He submitted several proposals for peace to the warring powers. While his suggestions were rejected, he held the respect of both sides. He was active in promoting works of mercy among the homeless and hungry during and immediately after the war.

Pius XI was Archbishop of Milan when elected Pope in 1922, serving until 1939. Leo XIII had been his mentor in a special way. Pius XI negotiated the Lateran Treaty with Italy, whereby Vatican City was established as a state, with the Pope as temporal ruler. He ordered a radio station installed in the Vatican, and began mass communication with this medium. He wrote many encyclicals, including *Quadragesimo Anno* (*Reconstructing the Social Order*), 1931, or forty years after his friend, Leo XIII, published one, *Rerum Novarum* (*On the Condition of Labor*).

Pius XII served from 1939 to 1958. As Cardinal Pacelli he had been Secretary of State under Pius XI, and in this capacity traveled to South America and to the United States, where he met President Franklin D. Roosevelt. Pius XII had to deal with the great problems resulting from the rise of Fascism in Italy and Germany and also from the spread of Communism in the world. In 1939 President Roosevelt appointed Myron C. Taylor, a corporation executive and an Episcopalian, as his personal representative to the Pope, but without full diplomatic status. This somewhat informal arrangement established communication between the government of the United States and the Holy See. Mr. Taylor stayed on after the death of President Roosevelt in 1945, and served under President Truman until 1950. No other appointment was made (see "Vatican Diplomacy" in Chapter 1). Pius XII worked effectively to relieve the suffering of refugees and of other persons destitute as a consequence of the war and postwar upheaval. He made numerous addresses by radio to the people of the world on the bases of a just and lasting peace.

John XXIII, whose career has been sketched above in the opening paragraphs of this chapter, was Archbishop of Venice when elected Pope in 1958. He had served in France and the Near East prior to going to Venice in 1953, and he thus saw at firsthand the social conditions that his Church faced. He became an unconventional Pope, communicating with a number of officials of other religious bodies, and authorizing broad dialogue between Catholics and those of other faiths. His writings and his call for the Second Vatican Council received the respectful attention of statesmen and religious leaders generally.

Paul VI was Archbishop of Milan when elected Pope in 1963. He had as Monsignor Montini served the Holy See for a long time. Pius XII wished to make him a cardinal in 1953, but the hat was declined. He was appointed to Milan in 1954. When he entered the city he kissed the ground there as a symbol of his love for the place and its people. Pope John made him a cardinal in 1958. He was one of the Pope's close advisers in the course of the sessions of the Vatican Council in 1962.

In his coronation address in 1963, Pope Paul said he would continue the ongoing dialogue. He also pledged to advance and implement the policies of his predecessor, and announced the reconvening of the Vatican Council.

He has always shown great interest in the welfare of the industrial workers, social reform, and international cooperation. As an admistrator he proved himself a pastor of people, a man of culture, and a diplomat. His personality combined piety, courage, tact, and gentleness. He visited Jerusalem early in 1964. There he conferred with the Ecumenical Patriarch of the Eastern Orthodox Church, His All Holiness, Athenagoras, Archbishop of Constantinople. This was the first meeting between such officials for centuries. In his first encyclical, *Ecclesiam Suam* (*His Church* or *Christ's Church*), 1964, Paul VI asked his Church to discover and state its true nature and to conduct authentic dialogue with the world. He established a Secretariat on non-Christian Religions, stating his willingness to have dialogue with them on the basis of mutual respect.

13

Ecumenism
as Official Policy

For many years prior to the regime of John XXIII, 1958–1963, efforts ecumenical in the Catholic Church were mainly the work of individuals and their associations. Indeed, the word ecumenical did not seem to have wide use. A priest of high rank once remarked of the period before 1958 that the word ecumenical seemed to be a museum word in his Church, and that adherents of the World Council of Churches, with Orthodox and Protestant constituencies, seemed to find more significance in the word. Although there are at least seven meanings of the word ecumenical, it is used here to designate worldwide movements for attaining understanding, cooperation, and unity among the various religious bodies.

Then came Pope John with his announcement early in 1959 that he would convene an Ecumenical Council. It was soon named the Second Vatican Council, because it followed one held there in 1869–1870. The Council would bring together the bishops of the Church, some 2,500 in number, as voting members. The discussions in connection with the preparations and during the sessions received wide publicity, which put the word ecumenical into the widest circulation in modern times. The Council would, the Pope said, be mainly concerned with internal affairs of the Catholic Church, but indirectly there might be contributions to the search for unity with Eastern Orthodox and Protestant bodies. As the "schema" or agenda developed it was soon evident that the Pope had as his objective *aggiornamento,* or updating or modernizing the relation of the Church with the world. And the world obviously included the Eastern Orthodox and the Protestants.

Secretariat for Promoting Christian Unity

During the preparations for the Council, the Pope established a new Secretariat for Promoting Christian Unity. As its president he appointed Augustin Cardinal Bea, S.J., the only cardinal who is also a Jesuit. Cardinal Bea, a German, lost no time in promoting Christian unity. The staff of the Secretariat conferred informally with both Orthodox and Protestant officials. The Cardinal soon learned that Protestant officials were generally respectful and interested in the forthcoming Council, an attitude far different from that of 1869–1870. The Orthodox were plainly more reserved. One of the actions of the Secretariat was to send five observers of the Catholic Church to the General Assembly of the World Council of Churches, held in New Delhi, India, November–December, 1961. That Assembly, representative of some two hundred church bodies in many nations, warmly welcomed the Catholic observers, who attended the general sessions.

Before the Second Vatican Council convened in October, 1962, invitations went from the Secretariat for Promoting Christian Unity to the international agencies of the Protestant Churches, the Anglican Communion, the World Council of Churches with both Protestants and Orthodox, and various of the autonomous Eastern Churches, inviting them to send delegate-observers. Some forty persons accepted invitations for the first session of the Council, more for the second, and many more for the third.

They were given the agenda, admitted to general sessions, furnished with interpreters of the proceedings and documents in Latin, given periodic briefings on the progress made, and invited freely to express their views, favorable or unfavorable. It seems that practically all the observers made favorable reports to their constituencies regarding the warmth of the hospitality, the purposes and methods of the Council, and the information received. The Catholic officials, in turn, secured much information, opinion, and comment from the delegate observers, who were in some instances, e.g., in regard to religious liberty, persons of influence, even on a Catholic Council.

Thus it was established before the world that ecumenism was to be not only an enthusiasm of relatively few devoted souls but also the official policy of the Catholic Church. Non-Catholics, too, became convinced that there would be authentic dialogue in the form of exchange of information and opinion that could well lead to better understanding. And if there would be better understanding, there was good ground for hope that the search for practical steps in cooperation and unity would also be taken.

Numerous statements and events are now briefly summarized.

Baptism as a Bond

During the first session of the Vatican Council, 1962, Augustin Cardinal Bea, president of the Secretariat for Promoting Christian Unity, met with the delegate observers. Calling them "dear brothers in Christ," he said that his greeting to these non-Catholics was given with "profound consciousness of the immeasurable grace of baptism which has established bonds that are indestructible, stronger than all our divisions."

The recognition of all Christian baptism has been established by Luigi Ciappi, a papal theologian, citing as authorities Leo XIII and Pius XI, and declarations of the Sacred Congregation of the Holy Office. He stated in 1963 that "real Christians" are those who, having been baptized, have "supernatural faith in Christ, the Redeemer, and are united with Him through bonds of charity and respect for His teachings and precepts." He wrote that such persons, even in bodies separated from the Holy See, "live in a certain communion of supernatural gifts both with Christ the Head and with the members of His Mystical Body," and thus "benefit from the communion of saints, enjoying in part the treasures of merit, of satisfaction and of prayer which circulate among members of the Mystical Body." [1]

"Startling Improvements"

The following events and declarations in 1964 are illustrations of what many call "startling improvements" in the relations of Roman Catholics and Protestants.

Archbishop Lawrence J. Shehan of Baltimore told the annual Chesapeake Synod of the United Presbyterian Church in the U.S.A. that ecumenical movements had become possible because of a common realization that "there are certain basic beliefs held in common: the divinity of Jesus and hence, also, the mystery of the Holy Trinity; redemption through the passion and death of Our Lord; the reality of the Resurrection; salvation through the grace of Christ." However, it was also evident to him that wide differences still separate Catholics and Protestants. These include "the nature and structure of the Church; the meaning and necessity of the sacraments; the manner of Christ's presence in the Eucharist; the place of Mary in the Church; the role and spiritual power of the Pope." What makes the present movements hopeful is the change in attitude toward certain of the doctrines that separate

Protestants and Catholics. This has occurred "during our own generation."

Bishop John J. Wright of Pittsburgh asked the officers of the General Conference of the Methodist Church meeting in his city if he might deliver a message of welcome. The Methodists responded favorably. His welcome, said the bishop, was not detached, formal, and perfunctory. "It is the welcome of a neighbor, and, much more, the welcome of a friend." He thanked Protestants for the warm affection expressed for the late Pope John and for Pope Paul. This was the first time in the history of Methodism in the United States that a Catholic bishop had addressed the General Conference.

When Archbishop John K. Amissah of Ghana visited the Catholic Diocese of Indianapolis, an interfaith and interracial meeting was held at which Bishop Joseph Gomez of the African Methodist Episcopal Church in the U.S. said that the presence of a Catholic Archbishop from Ghana was an "eloquent commentary on the new day that has dawned." He said that the cause of ecumenism so nobly begun by Popes John and Paul was "resulting in a deepening of a spirit of interfaith interdependence."

In Cleveland 800 Catholics attended an "ecumenical hymn festival" at St. Paul's Episcopal Church.

Some 150 Catholics visited All Saints Episcopal Church in Indianapolis; earlier, men of the Episcopal Church had visited St. Rita's Roman Catholic Church. The exchange was arranged by the District Council of Catholic Men. There was exchange of information, not common worship.

A Roman Catholic parish in Tulsa, Oklahoma, became a member of that city's Council of Churches, which formerly had been representative of only Protestant churches. This was the first formal affiliation of a Catholic parish with a city council of churches in the United States.

The Catholic national newspaper, *Our Sunday Visitor,*

began a bimonthly newsletter containing synopses of materials appearing in a hundred Protestant periodicals. The editors announced that the "ecumenical movement requires that we not only speak but that we listen as well." Previously the *Visitor* started an edition named "Operation Understanding" which was circulated among Protestant and other clergymen.

A Benedictine priest and an Episcopalian clergyman officiated jointly at a wedding of a Roman Catholic man and an Episcopalian woman in St. Louis. The "exchange of promises" between bride and groom was read by the Catholic priest, thus meeting the requirements of the law of that body. However, both the Roman Missal and the Episcopal Book of Common Prayer were used. It was probably the first such event in the nation.

Publication in the United States and Britain of sixty volumes of St. Thomas Aquinas' *Summa Theologica*, a thirteenth-century work, should "further the dialogue between Catholics and Protestants," said Thomas C. O'Brien, professor of theology at the Dominican House of Studies, Washington. He is general editor in the United States of the series. The first three volumes were published in the United States in 1964.

The Jesuit Fathers in New York, editors of the weekly review, *America*, announced the establishment of the John LaFarge Institute, in memory of the late John LaFarge, S.J. The Institute is to carry on his work and advance his ideals, which included the organization of local Catholic interracial councils, and encouragement of ecumenical movements. There were earlier times when Father LaFarge seemed one of the lonely pioneers.

Webster College, a Roman Catholic institution in St. Louis, appointed two theologians of the United Church of Christ to the faculty as part-time lecturers. They are Elmer J. Arndt and Walter J. Brueggeman, both professors at Eden Theological Seminary, located near St. Louis.

Archbishop James Peter Davis of Santa Fe, New Mexico, announced that the archdiocese would become a member of the New Mexico Council of Churches, of which seven Protestant bodies in that state had been the only members. The Council is a cooperative body consisting of clergy and laity from each of the churches represented.

In 1965:

The Roman Catholic bishops of the United States appointed a national commission to implement the recommendations of the Second Vatican Council on ecumenism.

The National Lutheran Council of the United States, representing two large Lutheran denominations, voted to initiate formal discussions with Roman Catholics with the aim of mutual understanding and cooperation.

Four Catholic dioceses in Indiana cooperated with the Indiana Council of Churches, with a Protestant constituency, in the incorporation of Associated Migrant Opportunity Services, an organization which will carry on programs of education, child care, and social service among the seasonal farm workers in that state.

The Central Committee of the World Council of Churches, representing 208 Protestant and Orthodox bodies in 80 nations, including the United States, appointed a "working party" to explore dialogue with Roman Catholic leaders. The step was greeted with approval by the Vatican Commission for Promotion of Christian Unity, which sent representatives to Geneva for the first meeting.

Week of Prayer for Christian Unity

For some years Roman Catholics, Eastern Orthodox, and Protestants of many nations have all observed the days, January 18–25, as a "Week of Prayer for Christian

Unity." This has been one of the few times of simultaneous observance. Prayers are usually offered in separate houses of worship, but some Protestants have held union services. Judging by some of the reports of the "weeks," there are in Catholic circles prayers for personal holiness, for renewal of the Church, for the unity that God wills, for love and understanding of those who differ. There are also Catholics who pray mainly that the separated brethren shall return to allegiance to the Holy See.

A Unique Gathering

At Montreal, Canada, as part of the fourth World Conference on Faith and Order convened by the World Council of Churches, an unprecedented ecumenical session was held in the summer of 1963. There was no presiding officer and no pulpit. When the session opened, the platform of the auditorium of the University of Montreal was empty. Then one by one appeared the persons who took part. The Lord's Prayer was said, and there were brief addresses of welcome. W. A. Visser't Hooft, general secretary of the World Council of Churches, expressed "the deep astonishment one must feel at the character of the meeting." "It shows that a new beginning is being made." There seem to be unsurpassable obstacles. "But we all hear the prayer: that they may all be one."

"We are one in Christ," was the theme of an address by Paul-Emile Cardinal Léger, Archbishop of Montreal. The gathering of people from many religious bodies throughout the world was a kind of family reunion, he said. This was a sign of hope, however long the road to unity and its promise to the world. Among the difficulties he mentioned was that because of differences regarding the eucharistic mystery, "We cannot yet celebrate together the eucharistic prayer of unity."

Pope Paul's Pilgrimage to the Holy Land

Pope Paul's visit to Jordan and Israel in 1964 proved to be a very complicated affair diplomatically because of the current relations between the Arab States and Israel. It assumed great ecumenical significance, however, because the Pope conferred with His All Holiness, Patriarch Athenagoras, who is the Ecumenical Patriarch of the Eastern Orthodox Churches. Their conference was the result of long earlier planning. The Orthodox patriarch traveled from Istanbul to Jerusalem for the joint talks. The heads of the Churches of East and West had not met for centuries. This conference was probably the high point and possibly the chief purpose of the Pope's trip.

Relationships between the Orthodox and Rome have probably been as strained as those generally between Protestants and Roman Catholics throughout the world. The Orthodox did not at first respond as readily as Protestants to invitations to designate delegate observers to the Vatican Council in 1962. However, a Pan Orthodox Conference in 1963 authorized dialogue with the Roman Catholic Church. And the Ecumenical Patriarch, it is understood, had gone to meet the Pope in 1964 with the approval of at least six other patriarchs of the Eastern Orthodox Churches. Thus the talks in the Holy Land seem to have encouraged the Orthodox to undertake in a most serious and systematic way an exploration of their special problems in relation to Rome. These seem still to be mainly the phrasing of the Nicene Creed, and the powers of the Pope.

Pope Paul's First Encyclical

Pope Paul's first encyclical, *Ecclesiam Suam* (*His Church* or *Christ's Church*) was studied with much interest by those concerned with ecumenism in many church bodies. While he said that he was refraining from direct comment on issues still before the Ecumenical Council, he made generalizations regarding the Church, its relation with other religious bodies, and to the world. And these observations were obviously in the context of many of the deliberations of the Council.

Among many other matters in a document of 14,000 words, the Pope asked his Church to know itself so that it could effectively carry on a dialogue with the modern world, although there seemed to be no basis for dialogue with Communists. On the non-Christian religions the Pope wrote in part: "We desire to join with them in promoting and defending common ideals of religious liberty, human brotherhood, good culture, social welfare, and civil order. For our part, we are ready to enter into discussion of these common ideals, and we will not fail to take the initiative where our offer of discussion in genuine mutual respect would be well received."

As for the search for Christian unity, the Pope recorded that dialogue among Christians had already begun. He would only make a few comments, none of them new: "The principle that we are happy to make our own is this: Let us stress what we have in common rather than what divides us. This provides a good and fruitful subject for our dialogue. We are ready to carry it out wholeheartedly. We will say more.

"On many points of difference regarding tradition, spirituality, canon law, and worship, we are ready to study how we can satisfy the legitimate desires of our Christian brothers, still separated from us . . . The Catholic Church will not cease by prayer and penance, to prepare herself worthily for the longed-for reconciliation."

The Pope, like those of many other officials of religious bodies, declared his conviction that Christianity is the one true religion. And, in considering relations with the separated brethren, he expressed distress on finding that they—or many of them—regarded as the chief stumbling block the "primacy of honor and jurisdiction" of the Pope. Without the supreme efficacious and decisive office of the Pope, there would be no Catholic Church, he wrote.

However, he also said: "We should also like to observe that this fundamental principle of the Holy Church has not as its objective a supremacy of spiritual pride and human domination. It is a primacy of service, of ministration, of love. It is not empty rhetoric that confers upon the Vicar of Christ the title of 'servant of the servants of God.'"

He greeted all Christians "with love and reverence." He hoped that he might continue to have with them a "dialogue of sincerity and love." He prayed that the Holy Spirit would breathe upon the ecumenical movement. He greeted with gratitude and respect "the participation of so many representatives of separated churches" in the Second Vatican Council.

Secretariat for Non-Christians

The formation of a Secretariat for Non-Christians, with Paul Cardinal Marella as the president, was announced by Paul VI in 1964. Although at this writing no detailed program had been announced, the general aim was reported to be to implement the Catholic aspiration toward universality of interest. It will function as a parallel to the Secretariat for Promoting Christian Unity, with Augustin Cardinal Bea as president, which maintains relationships with Anglicans, Protestants, and Orthodox. This Secretariat also continued to be responsible for discussions of relations between the Catholic Church and Judaism.

The new Secretariat for Non-Christians was not only

part of the preparation of the Second Vatican Council. It began to gather suggestions from the bishops of the world on relations with Muslims, Buddhists, Hindus, and others. It was surely evident that the Secretariat was established with the recognition that spiritual merit and value are to be found in other than the Christian faith.

One of Pope Paul's comments to a group of pilgrims in Rome in 1964 was: "No pilgrim, no matter how far, religiously and geographically, may be the country from which he comes, will be any longer a stranger in Rome, faithful still today to the historic program which the Catholic faith maintains for itself of Patria Communis (Common Fatherland)."

A *Presbyterian Resolution*

Among various recent official statements of Protestant bodies on ecumenism, that of the General Assembly of the United Presbyterian Church in the U.S.A. in 1963 is here selected for quotation in part:

"The past ten years have been marked by unforeseen changes in relations among Christians of the major branches of the Church. An emphasis on our common faith in Jesus Christ brings more trust and less suspicion, more cooperation, and less conflict. . . .

"The United Presbyterian Church is grateful to God for these manifestations of progress in Christian unity—an objective to which it has been committed by tradition—and by consistent purpose and action through the development of the ecumenical movement. Therefore, the General Assembly encourages its members, ministers, and institutions, and agencies to join with others in a fuller expression of that unity which is God's gift in Jesus Christ to believers . . .

"In association with Roman Catholics . . . we should seek to cultivate relationships in the spirit, manner, and pattern appropriate to fellow Christians. . . . Fidelity to the truth as each understands it is a condition of responsible and fruitful ecumenical discussion."

Among the "guidelines" suggested were these:

"Informal and unofficial discussion and cooperation will be quite helpful at this time at every level.

"Readiness to participate varies from country to country, from situation to situation, and even from person to person. Therefore, we should be sensitive in initiative and in responding to opportunities for such association.

"To prepare ourselves for cooperation in social action we should be familiar with both the recent Papal encyclicals and the corresponding statements of our General Assembly, the National Council of Churches, and the World Council of Churches."

The Zenith on Ecumenical Policy

The high point in ecumenical matters for Roman Catholics was reached by the Second Vatican Council, which in 1964 gave overwhelming approval to a policy document on ecumenism. This said that there are three close links between Roman Catholicism and Eastern Orthodoxy, in spite of nine centuries of separation—liturgy, sacraments, and theology. Under some circumstances, the statement went on, Roman Catholics may participate in Orthodox sacraments, and the converse is not only permitted but also encouraged. The gap between Rome and Protestantism, existing for over 450 years, is wider, but the common links are in the Scriptures, and in devotion to Christ. "Common prayer" with Protestants is encouraged. The Council cautioned Catholics against "imprudent" zeal in working for unity with these two great sectors of Christianity, but recommended programs and activities in this direction. (For further detail see Chapter 14, "Second Vatican Council.")

14

Second
Vatican Council

John XXIII announced in January, 1959, only a few months after his election, that he would convene a Council of the bishops of the entire world. The Pope said that the thought came to him while at prayer. Apparently the Council was called by the Pope without much consultation with the Curia, the administrators. There is good evidence that a high proportion of the Curia were not anxious to have a broad discussion, and were "against" the idea. It was named the Second Vatican Council because the First had been held at the Vatican, 1869–1870.

The affairs of the Roman Catholic Church would be the main business, the Pope said, but indirectly there might be contributions to understanding with Anglican, Protestant, and Eastern Churches and encouragement of movements toward unity. During the preparations for the Council the Pope established a Secretariat for Promoting Christian Unity, with Augustin Cardinal Bea, as president. The cardinal, a German, is also the only cardinal who is a Jesuit. The Secretariat soon established communication with the international agencies and officials of the "separated churches," for example with the World Council of Churches. The Secretariat sent, with the Pope's approval, five Catholics as observers to the General Assembly of the World Council of Churches held at New Delhi,

India, late in 1961. The World Council also became one of the organizations that sent delegate observers to the Second Vatican Council, 1962–1964. (See also Chapter 13, "Ecumenism As Official Policy.")

Preliminary Discussion, 1962

The first session of the Council brought together some 2,500 bishops of the Church as voting members on October 11, 1962. There were also expert advisers without vote, mainly Catholic theologians, and some forty delegate-observers from non-Catholic bodies. These observers were aided by interpreters of the Latin used officially in the proceedings of the Council. Reliable reports indicate that a number of the bishops, who had been neglecting their Latin, were at times with less knowledge of what was going on than the delegate observers. The delegate observers were given the full agenda, were invited to attend all general sessions, were given periodic briefings by officials of the Council, and were invited to present criticism. The observers were asked only to use their own discretion when reporting to their constituencies.

The Pope met with them all in a very informal session. He referred to his experiences with other Christians in Paris after World War II, saying: "I cannot remember any occasion on which we were divided on principle, or that there was ever any disagreement on the place of charity in the common work of helping those in need, which the circumstances of the time made necessary. We did not haggle; we talked together; . . . we bore each other good will . . . There burns in my heart the intention of working and suffering to hasten the hour when for all men the prayer of Jesus at the Last Supper will have reached its fulfillment, 'that they may all be one.'"

After the session Douglas Horton, former dean of the

Harvard Divinity School, a delegate observer from the International Congregational Council, wrote: "As I looked at the tremendous pageant of the opening of the Council, I could not help wondering where, in the midst of this magnificence, could be found any good symbol of what the Church really stands for. The Swiss guards and the dignitaries did not remind me of Christ, nor did the gigantic dimensions of the spectacle—but when one's eye fell upon the focal point of the whole thing, the Holy Father himself, there was to be seen a kindly man who did not confuse the forms" with the spirit. John XXIII was the symbol.

Broad and intense debate was at once evident. This went on not only during the general sessions but also among all those who frequented the two large coffee bars that had been set up in St. Peter's Basilica. Bishops became acquainted for the first time with many of their colleagues. Discussions continued in taxis and buses, at luncheons and receptions. A high degree of "openness" was apparent. The Pope had done what he said he would —open windows and build bridges. The Pope also told the Council that he drew special comfort from the presence of the delegate observers.

Bishops learned at first hand about the vastness and diversity of the peoples of their church. The size of the Council was impressive when compared with the meetings of 1869–1870. Three times as many bishops took part in 1962 as over ninety years earlier. It was also significant that the bishops walked into the Council alone, with no assistants. They had time to reflect and to secure information to an extent not possible when they were busy administrators at home. It was also reported, incidentally, that the bishops of the United States were generally "much younger" than those from other nations.

The results of the first session were largely intangible,

because the formal actions on the agenda were few. Partly because of a much overdue pressure to talk things over, only four of the proposals on the agenda reached the Council for full debate. And not one of these four was fully acted upon in the two months of debate.

The "high point," so far as attention of the Council was concerned, was the discussion of the transmission of revelation. The center of the matter was the relevant weight to be given to Scripture and tradition, and the relation between the two. The matter was committed for further study by a newly appointed Commission.

The Council adopted only a preface to a statement on the liturgy, and a small portion of the document, fully adopted later, in 1963. The Council quickly approved a noncontroversial section of a statement on communication, which was then adopted in 1963. Both are summarized below in the account of the 1963 session.

The Council discussed only in general terms an agenda on the Church, which was taken up again in 1963 and 1964.

Despite the few formal actions, many persons sensed that the Council was to become one of the important events in organized religion in the twentieth century. Between the first and second sessions of the Council, Roman Catholic bishops in considerable number began to address meetings of Protestant ministers. One bishop said, on beginning his speech, that if he had been invited a year earlier he would not have accepted, but a year ago he would not have been invited.

Between the 1962 and 1963 sessions, there was recognition of the unusual influence of Pope John, also unusual grief on the Pope's death in 1963. His successor, Paul VI, was committed to a continuation of his predecessor's policies. Pope Paul also promptly announced that the Council, which had automatically adjourned on the death of the prior Pope, would resume in the fall of 1963, and that all preparations in process would continue.

Between sessions Pope Paul delivered an address to the members of the Curia. He said that reforms in the administration were necessary and that they should be initiated within the Curia itself. Among the changes that he suggested were more international participation and transfer of some of the Curia's centralized functions to the bishops who could today perform them better locally "without injuring universal ecclesiastical order." He also stated that the Curia should not oppose a proposal, if the Ecumenical Council approved, to have some representatives of the episcopacy associated with the Pope in exercising his responsibilities.

More Action, 1963

When the second session met, September, 1963, the formal work of the Council was much better organized. Revised rules speeded up procedure. Efforts were made, for example, to avoid speeches that were only duplications of previous utterances. A number of Catholic laymen were invited to sit in the Council as auditors and to participate in the preparatory commissions.

There were considerably more Anglican, Orthodox, and Protestant observers. Pope Paul met with them and heard Professor Kristen Skydsgaard, a Lutheran, say on behalf of the non-Catholics that the main differences were over the theory or doctrine of the Church, but that progress had been made in attaining mutual understanding. The Pope responded, saying in part: "Listening to one another, praying for each other, and after long years of separations, after such painful polemics, there begins once again love for each other. This is what renders this meeting memorable and full of praise."

The lives of the observers were again filled with activities. They had more opportunities than a year earlier to meet formally and informally with many of the bishops and their theological advisers. It also seems well established that at least one well-known American bishop, who had neglected his Latin, asked a Protestant minister, with a translator at hand, please to tell him what was going on.

Pope Paul in his opening address summarized briefly the four main objectives of the sessions:

"The knowledge, or if you like, the awareness of the Church;

"Its renewal;

"The bringing together of all Christians in unity;

"The dialogue of the Church with the contemporary world."

He went on: "The Church is a mystery. She is a reality imbued with the Divine Presence and, for that reason, she is ever susceptible of new and deeper investigation." He knew about the difficulty of all matters pertaining to unity of Christians, but he also recalled the comforting words of Christ: "What is impossible to man's powers is possible to God" (Luke 18:27).

The Council completed action on the liturgy and communication, and the Pope promptly gave them approval with decrees.

THE LITURGY

The Constitution on the Liturgy, as it is now formally known, declared that there should be efforts to obtain "full, conscious, and active participation among the laity." It required that there be a sermon with every Mass on Sundays and holydays. The people should be encouraged to commune more frequently. At the discretion of national conferences of bishops, the vernacular may replace the traditional Latin in many parts of the Mass. (See Chapter 3, "Liturgical Movements.") In 1964, the Liturgical Commission, which is charged with implementation of the Constitution, issued instructions shortening the Mass by eliminating a portion of the Introduction, the Last Gospel, and the final prayers, effective in 1965.

COMMUNICATION

The statement on Instruments of Social Communication was adopted with over 500 bishops voting against it because they regarded it as innocuous or at least without newness or freshness. It is a relatively short document. The Council recognized the potentials in mass media for spreading the "good news of salvation." All who use the media should "fulfill the moral code," should exercise moderation and self-control. Parents should guard youth from communications harmful to them, and should not let such elements enter their homes. Public authorities have special responsibilities in regard to the instruments of communication, and "should encourage spiritual values." Catholic people should actively support the good radio and TV programs. The Holy See should issue instructions and norms "for the guidance of pastors and people."

About half of the session was devoted to discussion without final action of the agenda on the Church. There was also incomplete discussion of Ecumenism, and on the role of bishops in the government of the Church, which are reported below in the account of 1964. Statements on Religious Liberty and on Relations with the Jews were not brought to general sessions for debate, much to the disappointment of the non-Catholic observers and most of the bishops from the United States.

Many Decisions, 1964, 1965

At the third session, which convened in September, 1964, the proceedings were conducted with a pace much more rapid than in the previous years. Women attended as auditors, and the Council thus broke the all-male tradition of centuries. The delegate-observers from Anglican, Protestant, and Orthodox bodies numbered some seventy, compared with forty in 1962. The various actions taken were probably of more general interest than those of the previous gatherings. The bishops of the United States became more vocal. They were especially outspoken when urging adoption of specific statements on religious liberty, racism, and relations with Judaism. As an indication of the venturesome attitudes in the Council, birth control was discussed for the first time.

In the opening address, Pope Paul noted that the Council had already "aroused great hopes," but also "some fantasy and dreaming, as if one could gather its fruits immediately." "The things of the Kingdom of God come only slowly and in silence," he said. He again urged the Church to discover and define its true nature and its function in the modern world.

To the delegate-observers, the Pope said he was "happy and honored" by their presence. They were not only more numerous than before; they were also more interested in the details and issues of the Council. He announced to the observers that he was considering the establishment of a special Institute on the History of Salvation, possibly in the Holy Land. "Pray with us," the Pope asked in conclusion, adding that he hoped the observers would communicate the best and the most accurate news of the Council to their large constituencies. The observers also appeared to have more direct influence on the Council than in previous years.

A small group of from thirty to fifty Catholic bishops voted "against everything" brought up, it was reported, because they did not wish to have a Council. However, most observers thought that there was a large majority that generally deserved the term progressive.

The final form of the Constitution on the Church approved by the Pope moves away from earlier stress on the organization. It emphasizes the Scriptural basis, the Church as a mystery, the Church as the whole people of God, a pilgrim body with the hierarchy as servants. This is now broad official policy.

MARRIED DEACONS

The Council approved by an overwhelming vote the proposal to authorize bishops to appoint married deacons, but only persons of mature age. Deacons, as stated in Chapter 1 under "Clergy," assist priests, but may not say Mass or administer sacraments. A shortage of priests in some nations was cited as an important influence on the large vote. The Council specifically declared, however, that young men studying for the priesthood, who are usually ordained as deacons before becoming priests, may not marry. The Council's action was approved by the Pope and included in the decree on the Church.

COLLEGIALITY OF BISHOPS

The Council voted by a large majority in favor of establishing a body of bishops to serve as a permanent body of consultants to the Pope in administering all the affairs of the Church. The proposed body was quickly called a "senate," which is probably a glib but not a precise term. The body would convene at intervals, and would have a position "between" the Pope and the administrators of the Curia. It is regarded everywhere as a sign of decentralization in the Church. Its actions would undoubtedly depend upon the present Pope and future Popes. However, it seems probable that a Pope would be guided favorably by a consensus of this group of bishops; conversely he might be unlikely to act contrarily to a consensus. The theory behind the action is that the bishops are the successors of the Apostles of Christ, and the Pope, the Bishop of Rome, is the successor of Peter, regarded by Roman Catholics as the chief of the Apostles. The Council's action was approved by the Pope as part of the Constitution he decreed on the Church.

MIXED MARRIAGES

Roman Catholic regulations regarding mixed marriages have been a major source of conflict with adherents of other religions. The Vatican Council considered in 1964 a draft containing proposals for important modifications. Instead of requiring an absolute pledge from both partners in a mixed marriage (Catholic and non-Catholic) that children must be brought up in the Catholic faith, the proposal was that the Catholic partner pledge to do this to the best of his ability. The Church has required that mixed marriages, to be valid, must be contracted before a Catholic priest, and thus has not recognized a marriage before another clergyman. The draft presented would have given discretionary power to a bishop of a diocese to dispense with these requirements, in unusual circumstances, in order that a marriage of a Catholic and one of another faith should not become invalid. The draft would also have permitted a Catholic and another to be married before a Catholic priest in the course of a Mass, a procedure thus far not permitted. The proposal received, as expected, strong opposition from the conservative wing of the Council. The Council did not take a final vote on the matter and instead referred it to the Pope.

LAITY

When the agenda on the laity came to the Council for discussion, a number of speakers criticized it as being "too clerical," and asked that the statement be directed toward increasing the responsibility and freedom of the laity. This involved one of the crucial issues before the Council, one that recurred in connection with other subjects from time to time: How much openness or freedom would the Council risk? (See Chapter 4, "The Laity and Their Organizations.")

The Council reminded the Church that it does not consist only of priests, bishops, and cardinals. God distributes his gifts to the faithful of every rank. All may contribute to the renewal of the Church. Thus the laity share in personal holiness, in witnessing, and in practical work. The pastors are instructed by the Council to promote the dignity as well as the responsibility of the laity. They should encourage lay people to undertake tasks on their own initiative. Also: "Let pastors respectfully acknowledge that just freedom which belongs to everyone . . ." These statements on the laity are all part of the Constitution on the Church, decreed by the Pope.

ECUMENISM

By overwhelming vote the Council approved statements on Ecumenism (worldwide cooperation and unity), which were certainly new and far different from the traditional anathemas hurled against other Christians by the Council of Trent and others since. Some observers went so far as to say that the Counter Reformation arranged at Trent had now been generally liquidated. The Second Vatican Council recorded its conclusion that both Roman Catholics and Protestants had been at fault in the divisions of the past. The majority of the bishops showed their will to adapt and revise past decisions of the Church. They recommended self-examination and self-criticism to members of their Church. They voted in favor of discretionary authority to bishops to permit joint prayer with Protestants under special circumstances. They sanctioned dialogue between informed persons among Protestants and Catholics. They resolved to work with other religious bodies in improvement of public life. The Council statement mentioned three important links of Roman Catholicism with Eastern Orthodoxy—liturgy, sacraments and theology; and two links with Protestants, the Scriptures and devotion to Christ. The policies voted by the Council were approved by the Pope in a decree on Ecumenism.

RELATIONS WITH JEWS AND OTHER NON-CHRISTIANS

American bishops in large numbers made a big issue of the statement proposed on the Church's position on relations with the Jews. This had political overtones because of the antipathy between the Arab States and Israel. Catholic officials favoring a statement said, however, that they were dealing with religion and not politics. The proposed statement was not brought to a vote in 1963. In 1964, it again proved to be one of the more controversial documents.

The main point, as revealed by the general preliminary debate, was whether the Jews of all time, or only the present people should be exonerated from "deicide," that is the death of the Son of God on the cross. There is undoubtedly some sentiment among Christians that even the Jews of today have some responsibility for the killing of Christ. In 1965, deicide was deleted from the text.

The statement of the Council on the Jews, approved by preliminary vote, affirmed that the roots of Christianity are in Judaism, and that Mary, Jesus, and the early Apostles were Jews. Further, that the Passion of Christ on the cross was an atonement for the sins of all mankind, and that no special guilt for his death attaches to the Jews of his day or of this day. The declaration further emphasized the brotherhood of man, and urged all Christians to avoid discrimination because of race, color, or creed. It asked that there be no teaching in the Church to the effect that the Jews are a rejected, cursed people, or are guilty of deicide. On the sensitive issue of the universality of the Church's teaching, the Council quoted the prophet Zephaniah as expressing the aspiration that all the people of God would eventually address Him with one voice, and serve Him side by side with one consent.

The declaration approved by preliminary vote of the Council on the other non-Christian religions stated that the Church does not and cannot reject that which is true and good in these faiths. Mention was made particularly of Buddhism, Hinduism, and Islam. Of the last it was observed that the followers, usually called Muslims, share with Christians devotion and submission to God and expectations of His judgment.

RELIGIOUS LIBERTY

The bishops from the United States apparently unanimously called for a strong and specific statement on religious liberty. The heart of the declaration presented included the simple affirmation that every person has the right, privately and publicly, to follow his conscience in matters of religion. It was really a reaffirmation of what John XXIII had said in his encyclical, *Pacem in Terris* (*Peace on Earth*), 1963.

As on other issues there were schools of thought among the members. Some of the more conservative wished to say that the person in error deserved only the charity of the Church. Among those favoring a specific statement recognizing the rights of all persons, some sought to be only pragmatic. Most people of the world would probably agree that religious liberty is good—it works. (In the United States it has surely been supported by Catholic officials generally, for one reason because it has been good for the Roman Catholic Church.) Others wanted to hasten to do away with the often repeated accusation that the

Catholic Church is for religious liberty when it is a minority and opposed to it when it is a majority.

When it came to the "grounding" for the declaration, there were those who desired a systematic theological basis. They would say that according to Scripture the only valid act of faith is one that is free. Also, that faith is not simply intellectual assent to a logical statement, but is really the devotion of the whole person to a free union and cooperation with God. Others wished to stress the historical development of ideas and institutions, particularly the rise in the Western world of limited secular government. In other words, they wished to note that in this world the people are not living in an age of absolute rulers—the state had become depersonified.

In the preliminary debate, a statement on religious liberty in accord with Western liberal thought received wide support from bishops from the United States and Western Europe. A redrafted declaration came back to the Council only during the last week of the third session. The Council Presidents (cardinals) at first proposed that the members of the Council should themselves vote whether they wished to take action on the statement at that stage or not. Soon thereafter, probably as a result of pressure from the conservative wing, the Council Presidents decided that the matter would not go to the Council. This action sparked a protest petition, asking the Pope to intervene and order a vote permitting the Council to decide the priority. This petition, initiated by Cardinals Meyer and Ritter of the United States and Léger of Canada, received over 1,000 signatures, plainly a large majority of those then present. The Pope did not intervene. In the Protestant world, which is generally committed to religious liberty, disappointment was expressed, especially by those who had great expectations from the Council. Among the bishops in the Council, both "depression" and "resentment" were reported. In 1965, the Council voted nine to one for preliminary approval of a declaration of choice of worship in accord with individual conscience.

THE CHURCH AND THE WORLD

The long discussions of the Council on the Church and the World included such subjects as birth control, race relations, and the means of maintaining the peace among the nations. The general discussions of the issues surrounding birth control were conducted in secret.

Unprecedented appeals were made for the Council to engage in a searching reexamination of its traditional teachings on marriage and birth control, in the light of new knowledge in the modern world. Identical views were expressed by Leo Josef Cardinal Suenens of Brussels, Paul-Emile Cardinal Léger of Montreal, and Maximos IV Saigh, Melchite Patriarch of Antioch. Their pleas drew long applause from the members. The Patriarch of Antioch was quoted as saying that the Catholic norm on family planning (the rhythm method) is not being observed in a large majority of Catholic homes. The gap between official doctrine and widespread practice creates a major problem of churchmanship. Cardinal Suenens observed that official positions often resulted from "outdated" generalizations. Let us not be afraid to study the matter thoroughly, he asked.

All the American bishops present at the Council late in October, 1964, jointly asked the Council to speak out specifically against "racism in all its forms," and for the elimination of the cancerous evil of racial injustice. The spokesman for the 175 bishops then present was Archbishop Patrick O'Boyle of Washington, D.C. "Racism," he said, "is one of the most serious moral and religious problems of our times. If we fail to give it separate and adequate treatment, I fear the world will conclude we are insensitive to the plight of millions of innocent men and women who are victims of racial pride and injustice." He also stated that the problem of racism demanded close cooperation with Jews and Protestants. Bishop Andrew Grutka of Gary, Indiana, added that disadvantaged people "are looking to the generals of the Church militant for leadership . . . The Council must voice opposition to every form of racism with the force of the trumpets of Jericho."

The long document on the Church and the World received preliminary consideration in 1964, and there was much evidence of support for specific positions, especially on race relations.

MEANS OF TRANSMITTING REVELATION

The Council returned to an issue brought up inconclusively at the first session, the transmitting of revelation by Scripture and by tradition. Which of the two is the more important, and what is the relation between the two? There were two main schools of thought: (1) Let us take no definite stand, leaving the issue to time and further experience and study; (2) tradition has a broader scope of extension than Scripture, and through the further development of tradition there may be better comprehension of the mystery of salvation. The first position prevailed in 1964.

The Pope's Closing Address

The fact that so many bishops and advisers had spent so much time in Rome was itself "stupendous," said the Pope to the last session of the Council in 1964. The Church from this time forward will have a better understanding of itself. The role of the bishops in governing the Church had been redefined, and a group of them are now to serve as regular consultants to the Pope. In the next and final session, the place of the Church in the world and the issue of religious liberty will be declared.

The Pope praised the non-Catholic delegate observers for "assisting" the Council. He declared that Mary, the mother of Christ and the greatest of the saints, would henceforth be also known as Mother of the Church. He hoped that this would "orient souls to Christ and thus unite them with the Father in the love of the Holy Spirit." This last declaration was not likely to make for unity with non-Catholics of the world, in the opinion of consultants of the author of this book.

Several Appraisals of the Council

An "expensive and over-publicized fiasco," was the conclusion of a social critic in England. All that had been demonstrated was that the Church, as presently organized, was altogether incapable of dealing with the modern world.

The Roman Catholic Church is in a deep and serious crisis as a result of the divisions of opinion expressed in the Council, in the judgment of a prominent Protestant delegate observer who had spent time attending many sessions of the Council. This was particularly evident in relation to the issue of religious liberty.

The American bishops were "re-educated" in the course of the sessions of the Council, a well-known Catholic layman who had been in Rome for the Council sessions said. He observed that, unlike prior years, the bishops were now "ahead" of their priests. The American bishops, 240 in number, made up about one-tenth of the membership of the Council, larger than those of any nation except Italy.

"The most important weeks in the history of the Chris-

tian Church" were those of the third session of the Second
Vatican Council, in the opinion of at least one of the
Christian delegate-observers who attended. While important items on the all-too-crowded agenda did not reach
the final stage, the preliminary discussions and votes, particularly those on religious liberty and the Jews, were good
evidence of the prevailing progressive positions. Documents not finally approved by the Council, and thus not
issued as decrees by the Pope, were nevertheless influential on Catholic and other opinion in the United States and
throughout the world. These statements of "present under-
standings" will undoubtedly be considered locally and by
national conferences of bishops, and probably later by future sessions of the Council.

The Second Vatican Council thus assumed a most significant place in the life of the Roman Catholic Church
and in the history of religion in the world. The freedom
of discussion surprised both many Catholics and others.
The Council was also important because 2,500 persons and
advisers gave a great deal of time to preparations for and
deliberations of the Council from 1959 on.

15

The Roman Catholic Church, Other Religious Bodies and the World: A Summing Up

The Aims

Aggiornamento (an Italian word meaning updating or modernizing) of the Roman Catholic Church is often declared to be the chief end sought by Pope John and others these latter years. Others speak of searches for openness, renewal, unities. Pope John's words "holy liberty" are put forth as one of the great aims. Rediscovery by the Church of its true nature so that it can engage in true dialogue with the world is another purpose stated by Pope Paul. Better relations with Anglicans, Protestants, and Orthodox, and with the non-Christian religions, have been sought. All these may be fairly regarded as broad objectives.

The Means

By what good means have these great ends been sought? They may be briefly summarized as follows:

1. Broad dialogue, or exchange of information, position, and opinion, with other religious groups on the basis of mutual respect. The new and favorable climate created by both Pope John and Pope Paul, and their own clear commitment to dialogue, have encouraged and relaxed both Catholics and others for dialogue.

2. Widely read encyclicals. Examples are: *Mater et Magistra* (*Christianity and Social Progress*), 1961; *Pacem*

in Terris (*Peace on Earth*), 1963, both by Pope John: and *Ecclesiam Suam* (*His Church*), 1964, by Pope Paul.

3. The Second Vatican Council. This Council, called by Pope John without general bureaucratic initiative or approval, carried on broad discussions of most significant issues. The press of the world and many non-Catholics interpreted the proceedings, and the various schools of thought. The ferment of formal and informal discussion has generated forces making for progress toward the objectives.

Changes and Developments

What have been the main changes and developments?

BIBLE STUDY AND TRANSLATION

The Roman Catholic Church has shown marked interest in Biblical study and translation. Protestant and Catholic scholars now use the same sources and techniques of translation. A Catholic edition of the Revised Standard Version of the Bible produced by Protestant scholars, who consented readily to the changes requested by the Catholic scholars, is being published in Scotland, with Papal approval. It is being made available for private reading, not for use in the Mass. This edition is soon to be distributed in the United States.

LITURGICAL MOVEMENTS

Closely linked with the deep interest in the Bible are a series of liturgical movements that are increasingly influential. Mass with major portions of the text in the vernacular is now permitted. The sacraments may also be administered in the vernacular. The entire liturgy now becomes more vital to the lay people taking part. A sermon is now required at all masses on Sundays and holydays. Catholic worship thus places more emphasis than ever on the Bible and on the personal experience of the participants.

BROAD POLICY ON THE CHURCH

There is now general official policy emphasizing the Church as inclusive of the whole people of God, as a pilgrim body with the hierarchy as servants—different from earlier accents on organization.

MARRIED DEACONS

Married deacons of mature age, who will assist priests, may be appointed at the discretion of the bishops, a procedure aimed at relieving a shortage of priests in some nations. Young men studying for the priesthood, who are ordained as deacons before becoming priests, may not marry.

RESPONSIBILITY OF THE LAITY

Broader scope and more freedom for lay people are being implemented. This has come about both because many lay persons specifically asked to be trusted with more freedom, and also because the clergy have begun to realize that under modern conditions more of the responsibility for the work of the Church must be entrusted to lay persons. (In passing it may be noted that a Protestant official observes that Protestant lay people in the United States have a high degree of freedom but are not zealously grasping their opportunities for action.)

DECENTRALIZATION

Decentralization in church administration and formulation of policy has been implemented. Among the steps taken are the recognition of the "collegiality of all bishops" and the establishment of a group of bishops for permanent consultation with the Pope with respect to the affairs of the Church. The consensus of this group promises to be influential in guiding all the administration.

The Roman Catholic Church is now fully and officially committed to ecumenism, or international efforts for inter-religious cooperation and unity. Ecumenical activities are no longer the enthusiasm of a few, sometimes lonely, individuals. A Secretariat for Promoting Christian Unity and a Secretariat on Relations with Non-Christian Religions have been established.

The Counter Reformation organized at Trent 400 years ago has now been liquidated, in the opinion of many informed observers. The Second Vatican Council was distinguished, among other things, for commitment to dialogue and cooperation with other Christians.

Forty non-Catholic observers at the Vatican Council in 1963 and seventy in 1964 were evidence of serious interest in and concern with the deliberations and decisions.

MODERNIZING THE LANGUAGE OF THE CHURCH

In interpretation of its theological and other positions, the Church is placing much less emphasis these latter years on the traditional scholastic language, or the formulations of St. Thomas Aquinas, which most of the laity do not read or study or understand. The Church is giving much attention to the best methods of communication with several large audiences: the faithful themselves, Christians in other churches, and the wide world. In this process it has made much use of mass communication media.

RELIGIOUS LIBERTY

American bishops stood for strong, specific action at the Council in favor of religious liberty for all. After hesitation in 1963, the Council in 1964 was not permitted to vote on a proposed statement. However, there was good evidence that a majority of the bishops favored a declaration in accord with Western liberal thought, and the issue then came up as the first item in the final session. The Council's declaration on the Jews and Other Non-Christian Religions was regarded as influential in discouraging anti-Semitic opinion, and as conveying positive Catholic opinion on the values to be found in other religions.

MANY ISSUES UNRESOLVED

A number of important issues are left unresolved, subject to further study and dialogue. Among these are the relation between Scripture and tradition in the transmission of revelation, and primacy of one or the other; changes of regulations of mixed marriage; and the church's policy on birth control, race relations, nuclear warfare, etc.

GREAT TASKS OF IMPLEMENTATION

Implementation of the Council's consensus remained a formidable task of bishops and pastors the world over, in spite of the good channels of communication within the structure of the Catholic Church. The Church probably has the same problems in this connection as other churches. Not every bishop encourages every zealous priest laboring for civil rights in the diocese. Not every priest is interested in civil rights.

TOWARD AN OPEN ORGANIZATION

No person can appraise with full perspective the events and trends here summarized. Many could agree with Robert McAfee Brown, a Presbyterian, who felt that when he attended the Vatican Council he had at least seen "the flame of ecclesiastical misunderstanding being extinguished bit by bit in Rome." [1] There was also evidence of unprecedented collaboration of the Roman Catholic Church with other bodies.

The changes here enumerated, and the discussions summarized, have revealed in the Church varying schools of thought, dilemmas, paradoxes, contradictions. And the presence of these, for all the world to observe, is characteristic of an open organization. The conclusion of this book is that many forces are at work moving the Roman Catholic Church toward an open organization.

Opening Prayer
Said at Sessions of
Second Vatican Council

We are present, Holy Spirit of God; we are present, conscious indeed of the burden of sin, but gathered together especially in Thy name. Come to us, and be with us: deign to enter into our hearts. Teach us what to do and how to proceed; and show us what we should accomplish, that with Thy help we may be able to please Thee in all things. Be Thou the beginning of our judgments and bring them forth, Thou Who alone has the name of God, along with the Father and His Son. Do not, Thou Who lovest order above all things, permit us to undermine justice in any way. Let not ignorance lead us astray. Let not the desire to please turn us aside from our duty. Let not bribery or favoritism corrupt us. Unite us, instead, effectively to Thyself with the gift of Thine Own grace. Grant that we may be one with Thee and that we may not deviate from the truth. As we have gathered together in Thy name, so may we maintain in all things a proper piety and a fitting moderation that here our thinking may not fail Thee in any way and that hereafter we may obtain the reward of eternal life for the faithful fulfillment of our responsibilities. AMEN.

Official Statistics

Roman Catholics in the fifty states of the United States and members of the armed and diplomatic services abroad and their families, numbered 45,640,619 persons, *The Official Catholic Directory* for 1965 reported. The total represented an increase of 13,064,917 persons or 40 percent over the number ten years earlier; and an increase of 766,248, or 1.7 percent, over the previous year. The following digest of the official statistics is here given with the permission of Thomas B. Kenedy, of P. J. Kenedy and Sons, New York, editor and publisher of the *Directory*.

There were 28 archdioceses in the United States with a Catholic population of 19,688,115, and 120 dioceses, with 25,952,504. The figures include 2,000,000 persons (mainly members of the armed and diplomatic services and their families) reported living abroad by the Military Ordinariate.

Seven archdioceses each with Catholic populations in excess of 1,000,000 were: Chicago with 2,341,500; New York, 1,807,880; Boston, 1,783,139; Los Angeles, 1,581,015; Newark, 1,551,773; Detroit, 1,494,695; and Philadelphia, 1,324,853. Brooklyn was the largest diocese, with a Catholic population of 1,580,809. Others with more than 500,000 were: Pittsburgh, 916,214; Buffalo, 906,204; Cleveland, 853,148; Rockville Centre, 806,472; Trenton, 596,375; and Providence, 540,721.

Advances were reported by 129 sees; 12 gave figures indicating decreases; while seven reported no changes, compared with the previous year.

The number of converts reported to be entering the Catholic Church was 126,209, the lowest figure for a decade, during which about 1,500,000 conversions were re-

corded. The number of infant baptisms reported was
1,310,413, a decrease of 11,902 for a year. Marriages recorded were 329,450, an increase of 23,008 over the previous year.

The Directory lists 212 bishops, 29 archbishops, and 6
cardinals.

An increase of 1,304 in the number of clergy in a year
brought the total to 58,632, the largest ever recorded.
There were 35,925 "diocesan" or "secular" clergy and
22,707 priests who were members of religious orders.

The total number of unordained members of religious
orders was 192,325, of whom 12,271 were brothers and
179,954 sisters. These are mainly in educational, social
welfare, and mission work.

The number of parishes with resident pastors was
17,088, while those without resident clergy were 549. Also
listed were 4,447 "missions" in the United States, 1,406
"stations," and 12,344 chapels. At all these three types the
Mass was regularly celebrated.

There were 14,296 educational institutions of all kinds.
They included 117 theological seminaries operated by
dioceses, and 479 seminaries operated by religious orders;
304 colleges and universities; 1,566 diocesan and parish
high schools; 899 "private" high schools operated by Catholics; 10,503 parochial elementary schools; and 428 private
elementary schools. There were also 141 "protective" or
social welfare institutions for 16,300 handicapped and delinquent youth.

The full-time teaching staffs of all educational institutions numbered 198,756. There were 12,346 priests; 1,125
"scholastics"; 5,868 brothers; 104,314 sisters; and 79,103
lay teachers.

Students in the 117 diocesan theological seminaries
numbered 26,762, while those in seminaries run by the

orders, 22,230, a total of 48,992 persons studying for the priesthood.

Total enrollments in Catholic elementary schools were 4,566,809, more than double the number reported in 1945, the year usually regarded as the beginning of the current boom in school enrollment. Students in high schools under Catholic auspices numbered 1,095,519, again more than twice the total of 1945. College enrollments were 384,526, actually over four times the number of 1945. Seminary students of 48,992 were also more than double those of 1945.

The number of Catholic hospitals was 952, of which 808 were general hospitals, and 144 were specialized. The total number of patients treated was 16,895,603, which figure must have included many persons other than Roman Catholics. There were 341 Catholic training schools for nurses with 35,430 students.

Some Comparisons with Other Bodies

Data in the *Yearbook of American Churches* for 1965, published by the National Council of Churches, New York, containing information from all faiths in the United States, provide the basis for a few comparisons between the figures of the Roman Catholics and those of other bodies. The reports of most religious bodies were for 1963, gathered in 1964.

Roman Catholic membership was 16.1 percent of the total population of the United States in 1940: 18.9 percent in 1950; 23.3 percent in 1960; 23.8 percent in 1963.

Protestant membership was 28.7 percent of total population in 1940; 33.8 percent in 1950; 35.4 percent in 1960; and 35.5 percent in 1963.

Two hundred and twenty-four Protestant bodies reported 66,854,200 members in 1963; Roman Catholics, 44,874,371; Jewish Congregations, 5,584,000; Eastern Churches, 3,094,140; Old Catholics, 497,527; Buddhists, 60,000 (on the mainland of the United States). In each case the reporting bodies define membership. Most Protestant denominations enumerate persons coming to full membership at about age 13, although Episcopalians and Lutherans report all baptized persons, including infants; Roman Catholics enumerate all baptized persons; Jewish Congregations, Eastern Churches, and Old Catholic persons in the cultural or racial group being served; Buddhists report those related to their institutions.

Protestants have generally emphasized the Sunday school rather than the parochial day school of the Roman Catholics. The Protestant churches reported Sunday school enrollment of 40,983,036 persons, equal to about 90 percent of the 45,805,074 reported for all faiths.

Protestant bodies then reported 332,044 clergy; Roman Catholics, 57,328; Jewish Congregations, 5,070; Eastern Churches, 1,903; Old Catholics, 328; Buddhists, 90. (All these figures are for one year earlier than those in *The Official Catholic Directory*, 1965.)

Glossary

The following list of explanations and definitions has been compiled as a special aid for non-Catholic readers. When formulating the terms, nontechnical language has been used whenever possible. Various works of reference have been consulted in the course of the compilation. The wordings that are given are usually the author's summaries of Roman Catholic usage, written for a general audience.

Absolution. Pronouncement by a priest in the name of Christ to remit the sins of the penitent, after contrition, confession, and promise of satisfaction or change of conduct.

Advent. The first feast celebrated in the course of the church or liturgical year, in preparation for Christmas.

Anointing. The use of oil for anointing as a part of a number of ceremonies, originating in Jewish and Apostolic customs.

Apocalyptic. Pertaining to or in the nature of a revelation.

Apocrypha. A term applied by Protestants to a group of books of the Roman Catholic Old Testament; they are held in esteem by non-Catholics, and worthy of study, but not regarded as authoritative as the other books.

Apostles' Creed. The best-known and shortest of the great Christian creeds, dating in its present form from about A.D. 500, and traced to the so-called "Old Roman Symbol" of the second century.

Apostolate. Participation in work on behalf of the spread of the faith and in service of fellowman.

Apostolic. Pertaining to the Apostles of Christ, as the Apostolic or early Church.

Assumption. The doctrine that the body of the Virgin Mary at the time of her death was free of corruption and soon afterward was taken into heaven and united with her soul. The Feast of the Assumption is held on August 15.

Athanasian Creed. A formulation of Christian doctrine emphasizing the Incarnation and the Holy Trinity; probably not composed by St. Athanasius, but originating in his era. He died A.D. 373.

Atonement. The teaching that Christ by His suffering enabled the sinner to be reconciled with God.

Banns of Marriage. A public announcement of the names of persons intending to marry, the purpose being to discover impediments or objections.

Baptism. One of the sacraments by which with the pouring of water and administration of a ceremonial by a priest, the person is regenerated spiritually, and joins God's family. In emergencies, lay members baptize. Protestant baptism is now recognized if there is present the intention to do what the Catholic Church does when baptizing.

Basilica. A church of special significance, but not a cathedral (*which see*). St. Peter's in Rome, for example, is a most famous basilica.

Bible. The Roman Catholic Bible is a collection of 73 books, 46 in the Old Testament, and 27 in the New Testament.

Blessed Sacrament. Name given to the Eucharist (*which see*) to designate it as supreme among the sacraments.

Breviary. The book of prayers and psalms used by the priests for their daily private devotions, and meditations.

Brothers. The usual name for members of orders who are not ordained.

Bull. The most authoritative form of a Papal letter, in which the Pope declares himself first as "servant of the servants of God."

Canon. In Biblical and ecclesiastical usage, the word refers to a standard or a rule; applied to the books of the Holy Scriptures; also applied to a portion of the Mass.

Cardinal Virtues. The four principal or moral virtues, namely prudence, justice, temperance, and fortitude.

Cathedral. The official church of the bishop of a diocese.

Charities. The social services of the Church for handicapped, delinquent, neglected, and dependent persons, and for fellowmen.

Charity. The virtue that enables persons to love God, the souls in purgatory and heaven, and fellowmen.

Christ. The Messiah; the Son of God who born of the Virgin Mary became man; the Way, the Truth, the Word, the Life; the founder of the Christian Church. He ascended into heaven after His Resurrection and sits at the right hand of the Father; He is the Second Person of the Trinity.

Church. A word with many meanings, including a local place of worship or unit of organization; the whole visible company of persons who are Christians; the invisible "mystical body of Christ." It is by many Roman Catholics applied only to their own Church and the Eastern Orthodox Churches; by many other Roman Catholics the Anglican and Protestant Churches are also included.

Communion. See *Eucharist.*

Confessional. A small enclosure in a church building in which the priest hears the confessions of members.

Confessions. In Catholic teaching, confessions by members should be made once a year at least. The person confessing to a priest is expected to mention "mortal sins" and to state something about the circumstances of his action. Mortal sin is so serious a transgression that it may deprive a member of everlasting life in heaven, unless confessed and repented.

Confirmation. A sacrament ordinarily administered only by a bishop, whereby a baptized person (usually one eight years of age and older) is strengthened in grace by receipt of the Holy Spirit and assumes full membership in the Church.

Creed. A formal statement of the teachings of revealed truth; in the Roman Catholic Church the three official creeds are the Apostles', the Nicene, and the Athanasian.

Cremation. The burning of the human body to ashes after death. A practice generally opposed by the Catholic Church, but not absolutely or in all nations.

Curia (Romana). The agencies that assist the Pope; including Congregations, Commissions, Secretariats, and Courts.

Deacon. A person with duties of assisting a priest at the altar. He may perform other duties in emergency with special permission. After a period of service the deacon is usually fully ordained as a priest. In 1964, as a result of Vatican Council discussions, bishops were given discretionary authority to appoint married deacons of mature age, but unmarried deacons aspiring to the priesthood would still be required to remain celibate.

Decalogue, or Ten Commandments. A brief summary of God's commands to man as given by God to Moses and preserved in the Old Testament.

Dispensation. The temporary or permanent relaxation of a law or regulation. The best-known form is the occasional action of a bishop to dispense from abstinence or fasting on a particular day for special reasons.

Ecumenical Councils. Assemblies of all the bishops of the world convened by the Pope, with others attending as the Pope may determine. The decisions are of no binding authority until the Pope assents and issues a decree. There have been 21 Councils accepted by the Roman Catholic Church, while the autonomous Eastern Churches recognize only the first seven.

Ecumenism (or Ecumenical). Worldwide movements for cooperation and unity among religious bodies.

Ember Weeks and Days. The Wednesday, Friday, and Saturday following the first days of winter, spring, summer, and fall. Usually priests are ordained on these days. In early years, they were days of prayer for the fruits of nature.

Encyclical. One form of communication used by a Pope, concerning matters of major policy or position, written either to all the bishops of the world or to those of a particular country. John XXIII addressed his on *Peace on Earth* to all bishops of the Catholic Church and to men of goodwill everywhere, an unprecedented procedure.

Eucharist. The sacrament of bread and wine, a mystery whereby the true body and blood of Christ is received, and through which the grace of God is transmitted, punishment remitted, and charity strengthened. In other bodies it is usually named the Lord's Supper or the Holy Communion. It is traced to the last meal Jesus had with His disciples.

Excommunication. Formal censure or penalty by the Church of a member whereby he is formally separated from the family of God. The person excommunicated is still subject to the ordinary obligations of church membership. The penality may be removed by repentance followed by absolution (*which see*).

Extreme Unction (Anointing of the Sick). A sacrament administered by a priest to one seriously ill or injured by special prayers and anointing with oil. It is not only administered to one believed to be in danger of death, and the term "last rites" to designate it is now less frequently used than in prior years.

God. The Roman Catholic Catechism states that God is "the Supreme Spirit, who alone exists of Himself and is infinite in all perfections." God is the Father, the Son, and the Holy Ghost.

Gospel. The message of Jesus Christ to man as given in the New

Testament; also applied to each of the first four books of the New Testament.

Grace. The redemptive love of God for man, freely given; made clear in the New Testament as manifested through the life, death, and Resurrection of Christ.

Heaven. The state and place where those persons saved meet God face to face and enjoy eternal happiness with God and the saints.

Hell. The state and place of punishment for those who die in mortal sin, as required by God's justice and judgment—a deprivation of the vision of God.

Holiness. A personal state, made possible by God's love and grace, marked by a high degree of faith, purity, charity; union with God; often used as synonymous with sanctity (*which see*).

Holy Communion. See *Eucharist.*

Holy Orders. A sacrament administered by a bishop whereby persons are ordained to the priesthood and thus receive authority for many duties, including administration of the sacraments except for Confirmation and Holy Orders.

Holy See. The seat, place, or office of the Bishop of Rome, the Pope, the head of the Church; also sometimes used to designate the Pope as Supreme Ruler of the Church and those associated with him in administration.

Holy Spirit. The third person of the Trinity, of the same substance as the Father and the Son, from whom He proceeds and by whom He is sent on missions for the salvation of men.

Holy Water. Water first blessed by a priest and then used in a sacramental way.

Immaculate Conception. The doctrine that the Virgin Mary was from the time of her conception free from original sin (a teaching separate and distinct from that of the Virgin Birth of Christ).

Immanent. The indwelling of God's spirit and power within man.

Incarnation. "The Word was made flesh and dwelt among us" (John 1:14). God, the Son, the second person of the Trinity assumed human nature; His two natures, divine and human, were united in one person.

Incense. A burnt granular substance that gives off an aromatic smoke and odor, a symbol in a ceremonial of the zeal that a Christian should have and show.

Indulgence. Evolving out of the penitential discipline of the Church, indulgences are remissions before God of punishment through contrition and penance, granted by ecclesiastical authorities to the living by absolution (*which see*), and to the dead by intercessory prayer.

Infallibility. The Pope, when speaking as doctor and teacher of the whole Church, and when defining faith and morals, was declared by the First Vatican Council, 1869–1870, to have that infallibility with which the Divine Redeemer willed that His Church should be endowed.

Institute. A general term to designate the orders (*which see*) which have many responsibilities for the work of the Church.

Kingdom of God. God's reign as prophesied in the Bible; in the New Testament it has been manifested in the life of Christ and is still to come in the final victory of God in His world.

Law. Commandment of God as stated in Scripture and tradition; also used to mean the regulations of the Church.

Liturgy. The entire forms of worship as authorized and prescribed by the Church.

Lord's Prayer. Called by Catholics the "Our Father," *which see.*

Lord's Supper. See Eucharist.

Matrimony. The sacrament by which a man and a woman, both being baptized persons, enter into a solemn contract in unity and indissolubility. Decrees of nullity may under exceptional cases be granted by diocesan courts or by the Rota, a court of appeal, in the Holy See.

Messiah. The anointed and expected one—Jesus Christ, Son of God, Son of Man, Saviour of the World.

Miracle. An event that is the work of God, either independently of or apparently contrary to, the generally known processes of the natural world.

Missal. The book containing liturgies and prayers used by members of the Church for the celebration of the Mass.

Mortal Sin. A transgression so serious that it might deprive the person of eternal life; mortal sin should be confessed as soon as possible to a priest in order to restore the confessing person to the family of God.

Natural Law. "The rational creature's participation in the eternal law," according to St. Thomas Aquinas (quoted in the *Catholic Encyclopedia*). It is that general rule of conduct given to man by God, the Creator, within the forms and qualities with which he endowed man. It is universal, applying to all men.

Nicene Creed. A symbol or formulation of faith usually thought to have been first arranged by the First Ecumenical Council at Nicca, A.D. 325, and revised into substantially its present form by the first Council at Constantinople, A.D. 381. The subsequent addition of words indicating that the Holy Spirit proceeds from the Father *and from the Son*, beginning about A.D. 589 became the source of one of the main differences between the Churches of East and West, which finally divided in A.D. 1054.

Nuns. Members of religious orders for women, which are of several types, varying in accordance with their function, whether contemplative or active.

Orders. Disciplined organizations of the Church who live in community and engage in pastoral, health, education, and missionary work. Only the ordained men may serve as priests in charge of local parishes, and most priests in orders do missionary and educational work.

Ordinary. An official with diocesan or local authority; the unchanged part of the Mass.

Osservatore Romano. A daily evening newspaper, begun in 1860, published in Vatican City, often quoted in the press of the world. It is "semiofficial," but also frequently quotes texts of official notices and other documents.

Our Father. The term used by Roman Catholics to designate the prayer that Christ taught to His disciples, as recorded in Matthew 6:9–13, and Luke 11:2–4. In Protestantism it is usually called the Lord's Prayer.

Our Lady. The common expression when referring to the Blessed Virgin Mary.

Parish. The local unit of a church with a priest in charge. All dioceses are divided into parishes, the boundaries of which may be changed from time to time by the bishops.

Penance. A sacrament whereby the priest grants absolution of sins committed after baptism to one who confesses in sorrow and strives to amend his conduct.

Pentecost. A yearly feast begun by the Jews. It is celebrated by Christians in memory of the day when the Holy Spirit descended upon the disciples of Jesus, recorded in Acts 2.

Pope. The Bishop of Rome, elected by the College of Cardinals to function as the Supreme Head of the Roman Catholic Church.

Priest. One ordained by a bishop to assume full authority to conduct worship, administer sacraments, and administer a parish or carry on other work. Priests are of two ranks: Those of the second order may offer the sacrifice of the Mass and administer all sacraments except Holy Orders and Confirmation. Those of the first order are bishops who may administer the sacraments of Holy Orders and Confirmation.

Prophet. A religious leader who is a "spokesman for God," recalling the people to their true traditions and ideals.

Purgatory. A place and state where the souls of those departing life on earth in God's grace may satisfy divine justice for temporal punishment due for venial or minor sin.

Redemption. The deliverance of man from sin and death through the atonement of Christ (*see Atonement*).

Sacrament. A religious rite, a channel of grace between God and man, with two interrelated parts: a physical sign and a spiritual result or benefit.

Saints. Those whose holiness and exceptional qualities have been formally recognized by the Church. In prayer, the aid of the saints may be implored, but Roman Catholics, contrary to some impressions, do not "pray to" the saints—they pray to God.

Salvation. The attainment of everlasting life in heaven as a result of God's love and mercy, and of man's cooperation with God's grace in accord with one's talents. Usually this comes through faithful membership in the Church.

Sanctity. A personal state of a high degree of charity, purity, and faith, made possible by God's love and grace; union with God; often used to mean the same as holiness (*which see*).

Scriptures (Bible). The Holy Scriptures of the Roman Catholics contain 46 books in the Old Testament and 27 in the New.

See. An administrative unit headed by a bishop or an archbishop; the Diocese of Rome is called the Holy See.

Simple Vows. These are vows whereby the members of religious orders may retain ownership of private property, thus distinguishing them from the solemn vows, *which see.*

Sisters. A general term for women in religious orders engaged in health, education, social work, or missions.

Solemn Vows. These are vows taken by persons reaching age 21 who renounce both private property and marriage. They are to be distinguished from the simple vows whereby persons may retain ownership of private property.

Subdeacon. The lowest of the clerical orders, whose members are limited to assisting in the ceremonies of the High Mass. This order involves a vow of celibacy and obligation to recite the Divine Office daily. After a period of service a subdeacon may become a deacon and then a priest.

Synoptic Gospels. Those of Matthew, Mark, and Luke, so named because they portray the life and witness of Christ in much the same general outline. (*See Gospel.*)

Ten Commandments (Decalogue). A brief summary of God's requirements for man as given to Moses and recorded in the Old Testament.

Testament. A word that in Biblical usage means covenant.

Transcendent. God's power as prior to, above, and supreme, in relation to the universe that He created and rules.

Trinity. God in three persons, the union in one divine nature of the Father, Son, and Holy Spirit. (*See God.*)

Vatican City. A state in the western section of the city of Rome, established by the Lateran Treaty between Italy and the Holy See in 1929; including certain churches in Rome not in the same geographical area.

Virgin Birth. The teaching that Jesus Christ had only one human parent, Mary, a virgin, and that the Son of God was conceived of the Holy Spirit.

Vulgate. The Latin version of the Bible prepared by St. Jerome from an old Latin text, A.D. 382, and declared by the Council of Trent, 1563, to be official and authoritative.

Bibliography

The following list of references contains selections made from many available sources.

General Titles

Some of the more comprehensive works on the Roman Catholic Church are:

Attwater, Donald (ed.). *A Catholic Dictionary.* New York: The Macmillan Company, 1949.

Brante, George (ed.). *Catholicism.* New York: Washington Square Press, 1962.

A Cathechism for Christian Doctrine: A Revised Edition of the Baltimore Catechism. Paterson, N.J.: St. Anthony's Guild Press, 1949.

Catholicism in America. Compiled by editors of *The Commonweal.* New York: Harcourt, Brace and Co., 1954.

Davis, Thurston N., Campion, Donald R., and McHugh, L. C. (eds.). New York: The American Press, 1962. Selections from *America,* a review edited by the Jesuit Fathers.

Foy, Felician A. (ed.). *Catholic Almanac.* Paterson, N.J.: St. Anthony's Guild Press. Annual, 60th Edition, 1965. Distributed by Doubleday and Co., Garden City, N.Y.

Giese, Vincent J. *Catholic Church in the U.S.A.* Washington, D.C.: National Catholic Welfare Conference, undated. (Includes events to 1959).

Guardini, Romano. *The Church and the Catholic.* New York: Sheed and Ward, 1935.

Herberman, Charles G., and others (eds.). *The Catholic Encyclopedia.* New York: Encyclopedia Press, 1907, 1913. Supplement I, 1922. Supplement II, the Gilmary Society, New York, 1951.

Historical Statistics of the United States: Colonial Times to 1957. Washington, D.C.: U.S. Bureau of the Census, 1960.

Nevins, Albert J. (ed.). *Maryknoll Catholic Dictionary.* New York: Grosset and Dunlap, 1965.

Sullivan, John F. *Externals of the Roman Catholic Church.* New York: P. J. Kenedy & Sons, 1919.

Williams, Michael, in collaboration with Julia Kernan. *The Catholic Church in Action*. Revised by Zsolt Aradi. New York: P. J. Kenedy & Sons, 1958.

Literary Works

Day, Dorothy. *On Pilgrimage*. New York: Catholic Worker Books, 1949. Autobiography.

Fremantle, Anne (ed.). *A Treasury of Early Christianity*. New York: Viking Press, 1953. Paperback by the New American Library of World Literature, 1960.

Hazleton, Roger (ed.). *Selected Writings of Saint Augustine*. Cleveland and New York: World Publishing Co., 1962.

Joyce Kilmer's Anthology of Catholic Poets. New York: Liveright Publishing Co., 1937. Supplement by James F. Tobin. Paperback by Doubleday and Co., Garden City, N.Y., 1955.

LaFarge, John. *The Manner Is Ordinary*. New York: Harcourt, Brace and Co., 1954. Autobiography.

Merton, Thomas. *Seven Storey Mountain*. New York: Harcourt, Brace and Co., 1954. Autobiography.

Newman, John Henry Cardinal. *Apologia pro Vita Sua*. New York: E. P. Dutton & Co., 1912. Autobiography; first published, 1864.

Sheed, F. J. (compiler). *Poetry and Life: An Anthology of English Catholic Poetry*. New York: Sheed and Ward, 1942.

Education and Related Issues

Dawson, Christopher. *The Crisis of Western Education*. New York: Sheed and Ward, 1961. With programs of study by John J. Mulloy.

————. *Dynamics of World History*, ed. John J. Mulloy. New York: Sheed and Ward, 1956. Paperback by New American Library of World Literature, New York, 1962.

Fichter, Joseph H. *Parochial School*. Notre Dame, Ind.: University of Notre Dame Press, 1958.

Laidlaw, Alexander F. *Campus and Community*. Montreal: Harvest House, 1961.

Leclercq, Jean. *Love of Learning and the Desire for God*. New York: Fordham University Press, 1961. Paperback reprint by New American Library of World Literature, New York, 1962.

Newman, John Henry Cardinal. *Scope and Nature of University Education.* New York: E. P. Dutton & Co., 1958. Reprint of text published about a century earlier.

O'Dea, Thomas F. *American Catholic Dilemma.* New York: Sheed and Ward, 1958. Paperback by New American Library of World Literature, New York, 1962.

Social Teachings and Issues

Coady, M. M. *Masters of Their Own Destiny.* New York: Harper and Brothers, 1939.

Cronin, John F. *Catholic Social Action.* Milwaukee: Bruce Publishing Co., 1948.

————. *Social Principles and Economic Life.* Milwaukee: Bruce Publishing Co., 1959.

Fremantle, Anne (ed.). *Papal Encyclicals in Their Historical Context.* New York: New American Library of World Literature, 1956.

Gremilion, Joseph. *Catholic Movement of Employers and Managers.* Rome: Gregorian University Press, 1961.

Huber, Raphael M. (ed.). *Our Bishops Speak.* Milwaukee: Bruce Publishing Co., 1952. Texts of official statements of American bishops, 1919–51.

John XXIII, Pope. *Mater et Magistra (Christianity and Social Progress).* Washington, D.C.: National Catholic Welfare Conference, 1961.

————. *Pacem in Terris (Peace on Earth).* Washington, D.C.: National Catholic Welfare Conference, 1963.

Leonard, Joseph T. *Theology and Race Relations.* Milwaukee: Bruce Publishing Co., 1963.

Manifesto on Rural Life. National Catholic Rural Life Conference. Milwaukee: Bruce Publishing Co., 1939.

Masse, Benjamin. *Justice for All.* Milwaukee: Bruce Publishing Co., 1964.

The Laity

Callahan, Daniel. *Mind of the Catholic Layman.* New York: Charles Scribner's Sons, 1963.

Congar, Yves. *Lay People in the Church.* Westminster, Md.: The Newman Press, 1959.

Greene, Michael J. *Laymen and the Council.* Springfield, Ill.: Templegate Press, 1964.

Ward, Leo R. *Catholic Life, U.S.A.: Contemporary Lay Movements.* St. Louis: B. Herder Book Co., 1959.

Second Vatican Council

Releases to the press by the National Catholic Welfare Conference, Washington, have been invaluable sources. Excellent reporting of the Vatican Council, and many issues related thereto, have appeared in diocesan papers, for example, in *The Criterion,* official newspaper of the Archdiocese of Indianapolis, Ind.

Brown, Robert McAfee. *Observer in Rome.* New York: Doubleday and Co., 1964.

Küng, Hans. *Council, Reform and Reunion.* New York: Sheed and Ward, 1962.

Küng, Hans, Congar, Yves, and O'Hanlon, Daniel (eds.). *Council Speeches of Vatican II.* Glen Rock, N.J.: The Paulist Press, 1964.

Nelson, Claud D. *The Vatican Council and All Christians.* New York: Association Press, 1962.

Ecumenism

Baum, Gregory. *That They May All Be One.* Westminster, Md.: The Newman Press, 1958.

Bea, Augustin Cardinal. *Unity in Freedom.* New York and Evanston: Harper and Row, 1964.

―――. Unity of Christians. New York: Herder and Herder, 1963.

Boyer, Charles. *Christian Unity.* New York: Hawthorn Book Publishers, 1962.

Brown, Robert McAfee and Weigel, Gustave. *An American Dialogue.* Garden City, N.Y.: Doubleday and Co., 1960. Paperback, 1962.

O'Brien, John (ed.). *Steps to Christian Unity.* New York: Doubleday and Co., 1964.

Tavard, George H. *Two Centuries of Ecumenism: The Search for Unity.* Notre Dame, Ind.: Fides Publishers, 1960. Paperback reprint by New American Library of World Literature, New York, 1962.

Weigel, Gustave. *Catholic Primer on the Ecumenical Movement.* Westminster, Md.: The Newman Press, 1957.

Relevant Titles by Protestant Authors

Béguin, Olivier. *Roman Catholicism and the Bible*. New York: Association Press, 1963.

Brown, William Adams. *The Church Catholic and Protestant*. New York: Charles Scribner's Sons, 1935.

Fagley, Richard M. *The Population Explosion and Christian Responsibility*. New York: Oxford University Press, 1960.

Pelikan, Jaroslav. *The Riddle of Roman Catholicism*. New York and Nashville: Abingdon Press, 1959.

Rodger, P. C. and Vischer, L. (eds.). *Fourth World Conference on Faith and Order*. New York: Association Press, 1964.

Stuber, Stanley I. *Primer on Roman Catholicism for Protestants*. New York: Association Press, 1953; rev. ed., 1960.

Notes

CHAPTER 1

[1] Robert A. Graham, *Vatican Diplomacy* (Princeton, N.J.: Princeton University Press, 1959).

CHAPTER 2

[1] *Theologie der Gegenwart in Auswahl* (Frankfurt: 1962).
[2] Quoted in Olivier Béguin, *Roman Catholicism and the Bible* (New York: Association Press, 1963).
[3] Béguin, *op. cit.*
[4] See *Yearbook of American Churches* (New York: National Council of Churches, 1964).
[5] (Collegeville, Minn.: Liturgical Press, 1963).

CHAPTER 3

[1] Hugo H. Hoever, *I Pray the Mass* (Catholic Book Publishing Co., 1942).

CHAPTER 4

[1] *America* magazine (New York), June 10, 1961.
[2] Daniel Callahan, *The Mind of the Catholic Layman* (New York: Charles Scribner's Sons, 1963).
[3] In *The Commonweal* (New York), December 20, 1963.

CHAPTER 6

[1] *The Criterion* (Indianapolis), June 26, 1964.
[2] John C. Rock, *The Time Has Come* (New York: Alfred A. Knopf, 1963).

CHAPTER 7

[1] *The Commonweal* (New York), April 3, 1964.

CHAPTER 8

[1] *Social Work Yearbook* (New York), 1960.
[2] *Ibid.*

CHAPTER 9

[1] Anson Phelps Stokes, *Church and State in the United States* (New York: Harper & Brothers, 1950).
[2] *Ibid.*

CHAPTER 10

[1] Barrett, Dr. Patricia, *Religious Liberty and the American Presidency* (New York: Herder and Herder, 1963).
[2] January 10, 1964.

CHAPTER 11

[1] Quote by John F. Cronin in *Catholic Social Action* (Milwaukee: Bruce Publishing Co., 1943).
[2] *The Pilot* (Boston), August 1, 1964.

CHAPTER 12

[1] Quoted in Henry Cardinal Manning, *The Vatican Council* (New York, 1871).

CHAPTER 13

[1] From a release, 1963, of the National Catholic Welfare Conference, summarizing an article in *L'Osservatore Romano*, Vatican daily newspaper.

CHAPTER 15

[1] Robert McAfee Brown, *Observer in Rome* (New York: Doubleday and Co., 1964).